AN *Average* ENGINEER'S Diary

YOGEN SHAH

AN Average ENGINEER'S Diary

By Yogen Shah

© 2024 Yogen Shah. All Rights Reserved.

This book, including all content and materials herein, is protected under international copyright law. No part of this publication may be reproduced, distributed, or transmitted in any form or by any means, including photocopying, recording, or other electronic or mechanical methods, without the prior written permission of the author, Yogen Shah.

First Edition, October 2024

ABOUT THE AUTHOR

———◆———

Mr. Yogen Shah is a graduate engineer from K J Somaiya College of Engineering, Mumbai, and has built an impressive career working with prestigious companies such as Larsen & Toubro, IHI in Japan, and Petrofac in Sharjah. With over 30 years of experience, Mr. Shah has worked in various roles across India, the Middle East, and Japan, and is currently serving as Procurement Director in the Middle East.

Despite his accomplishments, Mr. Shah is candid about the fact that he considered himself an "average engineer" at the start of his career. However, through relentless effort, hard work, honesty, and integrity, he gradually climbed the ranks to achieve success in his field. His career has not only spanned decades but also taken him around the globe, allowing him to interact with a diverse range of cultures and nationalities. These experiences have enriched his perspective and informed his professional journey.

During the COVID-19 pandemic, as he found himself at home and missing real-life interactions, Mr. Shah turned to writing as a creative outlet. He began sharing his insights and stories on LinkedIn, where they resonated deeply with his network. The positive feedback from friends, colleagues, and followers was overwhelming, with many urging him to compile his writings into a book. Inspired by their encouragement, Mr. Shah decided to take the plunge and publish his first book.

In addition to his professional roles, Mr. Shah is also an active investor in the Indian stock market, a qualified financial advisor, a motivational speaker, and a seasoned supply chain professional.

ABOUT THE BOOK

"An Average Engineer" is a collection of short stories by the author, inspired by real-life experiences and aimed at resonating with the millions of engineering graduates in India.

Each year, India produces around 1.5 million engineers, yet only a select few from prestigious institutions like the IITs, NITs, and other top-tier colleges are regarded as the crème de la crème. The vast majority of these graduates are often categorised as "average engineers," facing the daunting reality of being perceived as less employable due to a lack of specialised skills or industry readiness. This has created a challenging landscape where many struggle to find their footing in the competitive job market.

The author, through this book, seeks to bridge the gap between these so-called "average engineers" and the successful professionals they aspire to become. The stories within offer practical advice and guidance on how to acquire the necessary skills to not only survive but thrive in today's demanding professional environment. The central theme revolves around a crucial question: How can one achieve success and carve out a rewarding career without graduating from a top engineering institution?

Leveraging his own experiences as a successful professional abroad—alongside being a seasoned investor, motivational speaker, and writer—the author shares valuable lessons on overcoming obstacles, building resilience, and succeeding in life and the corporate world. Through relatable anecdotes and real-world examples, "An Average Engineer" aims to inspire and empower the readers to redefine their paths to success.

PREFACE

———◆———

I have a deep love for reading autobiographies, a journey that began with 'The Story Of My Experiments With Truth' (Satya Na Prayogo) by Mohandas Karamchand Gandhi. Since then, I've explored the stories of luminaries like Dr. A.P.J. Abdul Kalam in 'Wings Of Fire,' Sachin Tendulkar's 'Playing It My Way,' and Ratan Tata's insights through various biographies. More recently, I've delved into the lives of global figures like Barack Obama, Steve Jobs, and the latest, 'My Life In Full' by Indra Nooyi. These leaders possess extraordinary talent and accomplishments, and while their stories are inspiring, they often feel distant from our everyday realities.

These are leaders with exceptional talent and calibre, and while we can draw inspiration from them, their experiences may not always be directly applicable to our own lives.

We often think that only famous people, leaders, or public figures have lives worth documenting, but this couldn't be further from the truth. Every individual carries a wealth of unique experiences, lessons, and memories that are just as valuable. These stories, while they may not make headlines, are rich with wisdom, emotion, and authenticity.

Writing one's own story serves several purposes. Firstly, it creates a lasting legacy, preserving personal and family history for future generations. While large events or historical moments are chronicled, the day-to-day lives and experiences of average people often fade away. By documenting your life, you leave behind a treasure trove of insights that your children, grandchildren, or even great-grandchildren can learn from and appreciate.

Moreover, writing helps in self-reflection and personal growth. When you take the time to recount your experiences — whether it's a personal challenge you overcame, a moment of triumph, or even a mistake — you gain clarity on how these events shaped you. It offers a chance to process emotions, relive meaningful moments, and derive new perspectives that may have gone unnoticed in the rush of life.

Additionally, stories of everyday people resonate more with others because they feel relatable. When we read about someone who overcame difficulties that are similar to our own, it provides comfort, inspiration, and motivation. It reinforces the idea that struggle is part of everyone's life, and success or contentment can come from perseverance, kindness, or simple human connection.

An "average" life is often filled with extraordinary moments — sacrifices made for family, hard-won achievements, quiet acts of courage, and love that isn't always shouted from the rooftops. These are the stories that connect us, that give us hope and help us feel less alone in the world. They show us that greatness doesn't always lie in fame, but in the way we touch the lives of those around us.

In essence, writing your own story is not about seeking validation or glory. It's about recognising the beauty, strength, and meaning in your own journey. Your life, with all its ups and downs, has lessons worth sharing lessons that can inspire, heal, and uplift others.

I've long wished my parents would write down their stories, at least for me to know which relatives helped during tough times and who made things harder. It would have been valuable to learn who really supported them when it mattered. But, that never happened.

As they say, "Walk the talk," so I completed writing my own stories — An Average Engineer's Diary. 99% people are average just like me. We are not celebrities or highly differentiated students who passed out from premium institutes like IIT, IIM, IAS etc etc. I hope that in reading it, you will find something that resonates with you.

I am deeply thankful to my father, who inspired me with his hard work and honesty, and my mother, who taught me empathy. I owe a great deal to my wife, who has always kept me grounded, and to my two beautiful daughters, who are my world. Finally, I want to thank my many colleagues, my LinkedIn followers, and the fans who have encouraged me to compile these small stories and articles.

CONTENTS

BANIA FAMILY 2
POST CARD 6
THE PICKLE JAR 10
GULAB CHI AAI 14
THAPPAD 18
FATHER'S DAY – EVERYDAY 20
SPIRITUALITY & ME 22
VAYA GELELI KARTI (VGK) 25
WOMEN -INFLUENCER IN MY LIFE 27
WAITING ROOM 30
ATTENTION SEEKING SYNDROME (ASS) 32
BURDEN OF EXPECTATIONS 36
KARMA RETURNS 38
WRONG PRIORITIES – DR KARVE 40
AN AVERAGE ENGINEER 42
CAREER – BEGINNING OF LIFE 45
LUCK BY CHANCE 47
GOOD MANAGER – LIFE SHAPERS 49
CHANGING GOAL POSTS 51
ALTERNATE CAREER 53
LOVE OF LOCATION 55
SLOW DOWN 57
HOME COOKED FOOD 59
I LOVE DIWALI 62

SCARCITY – A STRATEGY	64
DIFFICULT CONVERSATIONS	66
YEH DIL MANGE LESS	68
BRANDS & ME	70
SECRET OF FREEDOM	71
HOUSE OF HAPPINESS	73
CONNECTING THE DOTS	75
BOOKS THAT SHAPED ME	77
ECOSYSTEM	80
FAILURE – LESSONS IN LIFE	82
RISK – TAKE IT ON	84
RAT RACE	86
TIME AND PATIENCE	88
DANDHO – ENTREPRENEURSHIP	90
SUNNY SIDE UP	92
REGRETS IN LIFE	94
GRATITUDE – EXPRESS IT	96
POWER OF GIVING	98
COMMON SENSE	100
SHAPE IN OR SHIP OUT	101
HUMAN TOUCH	103
INDIVIDUAL GOALS	104
RESPONSIBILITY & RECOGNITION	105
PATIENCE	107
ETHICS AT THE HEART	109
BOSS IS ALWAYS RIGHT?	111
DIFFERENT PERSPECTIVE	113
TRUST – EARN IT	115

CATALYST - FIND THEM	117
ZERO SUM GAME	119
DISCIPLINE IS THE DESTINY	121
NEW ERA CASTEISM	124
GOODWILL OF NEIGHBOURS	126
FLEXIBILITY – KEEP EVOLVING	128
ADAPTABILITY – CHANGE WITH TIME	130
PURPOSE OF LIFE	132
LEGACY	134
SHRADDHA – REMEBERING OUR OWN	136
NOTHING – ZERO EGO	138
WINNING WAR LOSING BATTLES	140
EXPECTATIONS SETTING	142
PEACE OR JUSTICE	144
COACHING ADVANTAGE	146
HARD WORK – DO IT!!	148
EXECUTION OR STRATEGY	150
BIG BAKWAAS	153
FINE PRINTS	155
STEPS TOWARDS LEADERSHIP	157
COMPANY EXPENSES	159
POOR ENGINEERS	161
BIRDS & HUMANS	162
LESSONS FROM A LIZARD	164
GORI MADAM	166
UNPLANNED CHILD	168
WORRIED PARENTS	170
STAYCATION	172

EGO MANAGEMENT	174
LIFE – FROM DEATH POINT OF VIEW	176
WHAT MAKES YOU HAPPY?	178
PURPOSE OF OFFICE	180
FRIENDS & COLLEAGUES	181
ARGUMENTATIVE INDIA	183
WEDDING PLANNER	186
MARRIAGE MARKET	188
SUSTAINABILITY	190
VACATION – OVERTOURISM	192
LOAN (DEBT)	194
INDIA – INVESTMENT DESTINATION	196
FREEBIES	198
FINANCIAL EDUCATION	199
PARENTAL FAULT LINES — I	201
PARENTAL FAULT LINES — II	203
ELDERLY CARE	205
DUBIOUS PHILANTHROPY	207
VACATION TO EUROPE	209
BLAME IT ON PARENTS	211
DEADLY DEMENTIA	213
PROBLEM OF PLENTY	214
PARTNER TRAINING	215
SMALL BUSINESS	217
INDIAN PARENTS	219
MARRIAGE ANNIVERSARY	220
HUM DONO	223
CELEBRATION OF SILENCE	225

FOOD VS PHARMA	227
INDIAN EDUCATION	229
MICHHAMI DUKKADAM	231
MONEY & ME — FINDING THE BALANCE	232
KANJOOS	234
FINANCIAL FREEDOM	236
BAHUBALI RETURNS	238
PSYCHOLOGY OF FREE	240
SKIN IN THE GAME (SITG)	242
BUYER BEHAVIOUR	244
PERSONAL FINANCE — EMERGENCY CALL	245
HUMAN PSYCHOLOGY — NEWTON	247
RETIREMENT PLANNING	249
PERSONAL FINANCE	251
JHUKEGA NAHI	253
BANK OF FRUGAL	255
MONEY MYTHS	257
RETIREMENT	260
ART OF LOSING MONEY	262
JOY OF COMPOUNDING	264
FINANCIAL SECURITY	266
FINANCIAL LITERACY	268
RETIREMENTALITY	270
MY INSURANCE MISTAKES	272
REAL ESTATE MISTAKES	274
ONE AND HALF MINUTE	276
HAPPY RAMADAN	278
AM I PERFECT?	280

CHAPTER 1

BANIA FAMILY

I, an average engineer was born into a lower-middle-class family, where tradition ran deep, and expectations weighed heavily. From the moment I took my first breath, it seemed my path was already decided — I was destined to become a small time trader or shopkeeper, just like the men who came before me in this family. My brothers and cousins followed the same route, working in small businesses, embodying values of honesty, sincerity, and a profound reverence for God. Yet, there was one thing we all lacked: the courage to dream beyond our circumstances, to take risks that could have led to something greater. Our lives were not marked by bold leaps but by cautious steps, keeping us firmly grounded to our lower middle class status.

The struggles of the middle class are endless — a daily battle to hold onto the little we had. Survival was never guaranteed; we were always one medical bill away from financial ruin. In our small village, we ran a modest cloth shop, and from its meager income, we supported not one, but two families — eight children to educate, raise, marry, and fulfil all the social obligations that weighed us down like a heavy chain.

My parents were the epitome of hard work and love, but even their bond was tested by the constant worry over money. My mother, who came from a more affluent background, dreamed of giving her children a life closer to what she had known — a life where frugality didn't mean sacrificing happiness. She wasn't extravagant, but she believed her children deserved the best. My father, raised by single mom, on the other hand, had grown up in extreme poverty. He had learned to stretch every paisa until it complete value is realized. This difference in their outlooks often led to occasional tensions in the family otherwise full of love & harmony. In those days, marriages were arranged by fate, not by choice, and their contrasting desires were just another challenge they had to endure.

I witnessed their struggle every day, and it left an indelible mark on me. One day, when I was just 12 years old, I gathered the courage to ask my father, "When will we become rich, like the uncle who lives next door in our chawl?" His response was simple but life-altering: "When you start earning – Take responsibility."

That single sentence became the driving force of my life. It was as if all my family's hopes and dreams had suddenly been placed on my young shoulders.

I had always been a good student, but after that day, I became relentless in my pursuit of success. I studied harder than ever, often without proper guidance, because no one in my family had gone beyond a basic education. Everything I learned, I taught myself, holding onto the encouragement of my schoolteachers and my English tutor as if it were a lifeline.

I still remember the overwhelming pride I felt when I scored 87% on my 10th class exams—a record for our village school. This was followed by 83% in my 12th Science exams and then admission to an engineering college. Although I narrowly missed the top government engineering college, I secured a spot reputed private Engineering college, though expensive. I will always be grateful to my father for agreeing to pay the fees during those difficult times. I didn't ask for much, but I knew that, to him, this was the best investment he could make — an investment in his own child's education & future.

My years in engineering college brought a different set of challenges. I lived in a hostel full of smart, intelligent and few wealthy, pampered students, and my room was right across from a cemetery — a daily reminder of life's fragility. Engineering was no easy feat; it tested me at every turn, and there were moments when I doubted myself, feeling like just another average student. The third semester was particularly tough, with subjects like Thermodynamics and Theory of Machines pushing me to my limits. But I didn't give up. I studied for 12 to 16 hours a day, going over numerous assignments, books & sample papers, determined to succeed.

When I finally passed my engineering exams, it felt like the universe had decided to reward my perseverance. After initial struggle for 1-2 years, Opportunities began to come my way, almost as if by chance, each one better than the last. The pinnacle was being selected to work for India's largest EPC contractor—a dream job that opened doors I had never imagined.

I thrived in every role, not because I was the most brilliant engineer, but because I was honest, ethical, and, above all, incredibly hard-working. Even if I was an "average" engineer, I became an exceptional professional.

My journey has taken me from India to Japan to the USA and now to Dubai. When I look back on all that I have achieved, I do so with immense pride. My international experience, combined with an unrelenting drive to keep learning, has kept me ahead of the competition.

Today, I am compiling my experiences and my journey from as an Average Engineer to successful professional, investor, author and speaker. It is a testament to the life I've lived, the struggles I've overcome, and the lessons I've learned.

CHAPTER 2

POST CARD

It was the 13th-day ceremony for my grandmother, who passed away at ripe age of 85. All of our family members had gathered at our home for the religious rituals. After lunch, my uncle asked me to bring a few postcards so he could send letters to some relatives (since, in those days, phones were not easily accessible; let alone mobiles or WhatsApp).

I walked nearly two – three Kilometers to the post office. I was only 11 or 12 years old at the time. But when I arrived, the post office was closed, so I returned empty-handed. My uncle scolded me loudly for not completing the task. He even told my father, "Look at your son! You think he's a bright star because he scores 90% in school, but he can't even bring a few simple postcards!"

I felt terrible and cried. Even at that young age, I found it humiliating because I had genuinely tried my best.

The next day, I brought the postcards, but my uncle had already taught me two important lessons:

1. **Think outside the box:** Postcards aren't only available at the post office. They're also sold at nearby paan shops.

2. **Never return empty-handed:** Always complete your responsibilities. Be a task master. Good grades alone won't get you far in life.

These lessons have stayed with me throughout my life. Whether it's closing a multi-million-dollar deal for my company or buying coriander for my wife, I always strive to fulfil my responsibilities to the best of my ability.

You don't need to attend business school to learn management lessons — life itself can teach you through experience.

CHAPTER 3

THE PICKLE JAR

During my school days, classes were from 11 AM to 5 PM. We would go to school after lunch, and my mom would give me 5 paise for a snack during the mid-break. Naturally, as growing kids, we were always ravenous when we returned home after school walking distance.

One day, I came home feeling especially hungry, but my mom wasn't there. I tried to grab something to eat, but everything was out of reach. My small hands were not able to grab anything.

Determined, I grabbed a stool and climbed up to the top of the cupboard, where all the snacks and pickles were stored. Excited, I managed to grab a container and, in my eagerness, jumped off. In that moment, my shirt got caught on the cupboard's hook, and the entire thing came crashing down.

I was horrified. The mess was overwhelming — pickles, which were meant to last us the whole year, and snacks were scattered everywhere, completely ruined. I started cleaning up with my little hands, dreading my mom's return. When she finally came home, I braced myself for a scolding, but to my surprise, nothing of the sort happened.

As a matter of fact, both my parents have never hit any of us, me and my siblings. They were so nice hearted even not so much educated. Years later, I asked my mom why she didn't punish me for creating such a mess. Her response was remarkable, a lesson in leadership.

She said, "Even though you caused the mess, I was responsible for it. I should have been home when you got back, and I should have anticipated that you'd be hungry and set something aside for you. So in reality, I failed to foresee the situation, and I couldn't punish you for my oversight, even though it was a significant loss."

As a leader, do you reflect on who is truly responsible for the poor performance of your team? Do you identify the root cause of the problem, or do you simply punish lower-level team members, knowing they may be helpless to prevent it?

4 CHAPTER

GULAB CHI AAI

Everyone in the colony knew her as Gulab's mother. She worked part-time as a maid for our family, but also for several others in the neighborhoods.

She lost her husband at a young age. He had been a complete drunkard, spending his entire salary on liquor while alive. Ironically, after his death, it was his pension from the Indian Railways that sustained the family. In a sad twist, a dead man proved more useful than the living one. (This is one of the reasons I hate alcohol. I have seen many families getting ruined during childhood)

My mother treated her like a family member. Every morning, she would serve her hot tea and rotis when she arrived for work. I found it a bit puzzling, considering we were already paying her a monthly salary – why this special treatment beyond salary? As it is we are struggling to meet both ends. But for Gulab's mother, my mother was her **employer of choice! She will throw all other work and help my mother when needed -sometime ignoring other households.**

However, she repaid this kindness when my mother fell seriously ill and was hospitalised for three months. Without expecting anything extra, she stood by her side every day. She continued working for us for the next 20 years, while our family ensured that her children received an education and found employment.

My mother was indirectly teaching me lessons of **Empathy**. She was teaching me to **respect** people who were economically weak. We were instructed not to address her as 'Bai" or "Kaamwaali". Our maid was teaching me value to **Loyalty**. Honestly, kids learn most by observing what your parents are doing? How are they treating others, in particular weaker sections.

Today, such loyalty, commitment, and sense of ownership are rare on both sides — employees and employers alike. People who've worked for 20-25 years with one company, building their reputation, can switch to a competitor overnight. Likewise, employees who've dedicated decades to a company are asked to leave without a second thought.

Under the guise of professional growth, share holders value and survival, are we compromising basic human values?

Are you employee of a choice for your workers?

CHAPTER 5

THAPPAD

No, it's not about the Tapasi Pannu movie!

On October 30, 1975, our school celebrated Gandhi Jayanti. As part of the commemorations, we were required to observe a two-minute silence. I was a young boy, perhaps nine or ten years old, standing in front of the class facing our teachers. Our principal was directly opposite me in a classroom.

During the solemn silence, a mischievous classmate let out a fart, causing someone to laugh. I couldn't contain myself and joined in the laughter. Once the two minutes had passed, the principal chastised me for my indiscretion, standing as close as I was to him. I felt humiliated, my face flushed with embarrassment. In those days, teachers had the authority to punish students as they saw fit. The concept of child rights was virtually non-existent.

At a young age, I learned a valuable lesson: actions have consequences, regardless of who is responsible. Blaming others is a futile exercise. Whether it's your wife, boss, or anyone else, blaming them won't solve your problems.

Later in life, while reading Stephen Covey's "The 7 Habits of Highly Effective People," the concept became crystal clear. Covey emphasised the importance of acting within one's circle of influence. We have little control over others, but we can significantly influence our own actions.

The world may be grappling with challenges like the war, pandemic & climate change. We may have limited control over global financial affairs and prices. However, we must survive and fulfil our commitments.

A single slap was enough to impart profound life lessons. I've learned the importance of my actions and its consequences. Act within your sphere of influence. **You have no control over the actions of others!**

Today, while reading a psychology book, I encountered a poignant poem: "When I was young, I wished for courage to change the world. When I was in my mid-years, I wanted the grace to change my family and friends. But today, when I am old, I just want to change myself." Had I understood this earlier, my life might have been very different.

CHAPTER 6

FATHER'S DAY – EVERYDAY

I have not yet understood — why father and son relation in formative years is mostly complicated? For me father meant discipline and mother meant love. Our communication was very limited as he was deeply religious and after coming back from work he will devote time to religious readings. We hardly found time to openly interact and communicate.

But, most of the time, we only realise father's true contributions when they're no longer around. That was the case for me as well. Growing up in a lower-middle-class family in India, we had our own share of struggles. My father ran a small cloth store with his brother, and every day was a battle. We lacked basic amenities, kitchen gadgets, and furniture — at least until I started earning on my own but there was never a shortage of food.

What stands out is that despite all his hardships, he never wavered in supporting my education. He didn't understand much about higher education and engineering, yet he always found a way to pay my fees, despite his daily struggles. I don't recall him ever visiting my school, college, or hostel, but his support was unwavering.

My father lost his own father when he was just five years old, inheriting a heavy debt due to illness. He struggled to get an education but couldn't progress beyond class 7. He worked tirelessly until the age of 82, only stopping his work in the last six months when prostate cancer confined him. Even then, he faced the end with grace, without complaints.

He was deeply religious and worked 12 to 16 hours a day. Honesty was his hallmark, and perhaps that's why he wasn't extraordinarily successful in business, but he was content with what God had given him. He never complained, never expressed regrets.

I was with him when the doctor informed us about his prostate cancer. I was shattered—he wasn't. He simply said, "Bhagwan ni iccha", meaning "God's will." How could someone remain so calm and composed after hearing the word "CANCER"? It was because he was completely content with his life—no desires, just gratitude for what God had given him.

As a youngster, I never disrespected him, but I sometimes questioned his achievements and his cautious approach to risk. Once, I asked him, "Why aren't you more successful financially?" His response was simple: "What is your definition of success?" Define and find your own success.

It wasn't until I became a father myself, juggling family, work, and finances, that I truly understood what he had gone through. Today, I think of him at every stage of my life. I firmly believe that qualities like honesty and hard work, which are core to my success, are inherited from him. He is my North Star. If I can emulate even 10% of who he was, I would consider myself successful in life.

If you have your father with you, you don't need to look anywhere else for an idol.

CHAPTER 7

SPIRITUALITY & ME

My relationship with God has never been particularly close. To be honest, I don't have many strong friendships either. Most of my friendships feel transactional — when the need ends, so does the relationship or one can say 'kaam khatam – rista khatam!'

Growing up in a Vaishnav family devoted to **Shreenathji,** spirituality was a vibrant thread woven into my life. My father, deeply spiritual, would dedicate two hours each day to prayer. My mother, though not as devout, found joy in visiting temples—not for the rituals, but for the community and the chance to meet friends. She believed more in the goodness of people than in the power of God. Despite this, the rich spiritual environment of my extended family painted my world in shades of devotion and reverence.

As a child, I was captivated by the colourful images of gods that came in the mail as Diwali greetings. They felt like treasures, brimming with divine energy. I collected them with care, turning my cupboard into a gallery of vibrant gods. Each morning, I would greet them with a prayer, light a Diya, and experience an inexplicable joy — pure, simple, and without expectation. It was as though the gods were my playful companions in a world full of wonder.

But in 5th grade, life presented a challenge I wasn't prepared for. I was a top student, but a particularly tough math exam threatened to topple my standing. In desperation, I turned to God, pleading for help and promising to double my prayers if I succeeded. But nothing changed—my prayers went unanswered, and my marks reflected it. I lost top score in the class.

From that day till today – I have understood – you must rely on your own efforts. God will not help you. I had to rely on myself. It wasn't that God had abandoned me; I simply understood that God wasn't there to manage the daily challenges I once sought help for. No more prayers for exams, jobs, or material things. I stopped outsourcing my worries to God.

Does that mean I lost faith in God? Not at all. Life continued to surprise me, and there have been three distinct moments when I felt a higher power protecting me.

- The first was when I was driving on American roads for the first time, speeding at 80 miles per hour. With only my Indian driving experience, I suddenly lost control of the car. It veered into another lane, and just when a collision seemed certain, the car in the other lane swerved away — as if guided by an unseen hand. In that miraculous moment, we were all saved.

- The second time was on a flight from Tokyo to Indonesia. We were cruising smoothly at 30,000 feet when, out of nowhere, the plane plummeted to 3000 feet. It was a terrifying drop, but somehow, we survived. I sat there, stunned and grateful, wondering what force had saved us from disaster.

- The third time was on a journey from Baroda to Kolkata on the Howrah Express. I had stepped off the train for a moment, and as I rushed back, the train started to move. The platform was slick with water, and I nearly slipped under the train. Just as panic gripped me, something stopped me in my tracks. I stood there, breathless, feeling the unmistakable presence of divine intervention.

As I've grown older, I've come to understand how little control we truly have over life. So much remains beyond our grasp, filled with mystery and surprise. Today, I find peace in my daily prayers, spending 15-20 minutes in quiet reflection, focusing on my breath, and grounding myself in the present moment. This practice not only calms me but fosters daily introspection and a deeper connection to the divine.

Now, I no longer pray for personal desires. Instead, I pray for things beyond my control—health, safety, and well-being. Especially when I land in India, I am reminded of the joyful chaos that seems to be held together by divine grace. It's as if this country is guided by God's own hand, a source of constant awe and wonder.

In truth, my prayers have evolved from being personal to universal. I now pray less for myself and more for the well-being of my country, my planet, my world and whole of humanity.

CHAPTER 8

VAYA GELELI KARTI (VGK)

Yesterday, I met Anjali, my next-door neighbour during my childhood in a middle-class chawl in India during the late 1980s and early 1990s. She was a strikingly beautiful girl, but being ten years older, I simply called her "Didi" (older sister). Anjali's life was far from easy. Her father, an alcoholic, sent her away to a hostel to avoid the negative environment at home. When she returned, her hair was chopped into a bob cut, a bold move for that time. After completing her B.Com, she struggled to secure a job in a bank, so she took a receptionist job at a local hotel. Eventually, she joined the Taj hotel, where she worked late shifts and often returned home at odd hours.

In the conservative environment of our chawl, Anjali's choices were frowned upon. She was quickly branded a "VGK" — a derogatory term used to label her as a "bad girl." The community began whispering behind her back, questioning her character, her late-night returns, and her choice of profession. The more independent she became, the more she was judged. Few dared to speak with her directly, but everyone had something to say about her life. Her relationships, too, were scrutinised. She once brought home a Gujarati boyfriend, and after their breakup, she eventually married another man from Goa.

Fast forward to today, and Anjali is happily married, has two children, and she and her husband own three restaurants and bars in Goa. As I reflect on her journey, I realise how much the world has changed. Today, many young women possess the very traits Anjali was judged for — short hair, independent careers, coming home late due to work, and making bold personal choices.

So, was Anjali ever really a "bad girl"? Or was she simply ahead of her time?

Her story serves as a powerful reminder that we are often too quick to judge people without fully understanding their circumstances. We see behaviours that don't conform to our expectations and rush to label them, often unfairly. In truth, the traits we condemn in others may very well be the qualities that define their strength and resilience. Anjali wasn't the problem — society's narrow view of what was "acceptable" was.

Before passing judgment, we must remind ourselves that everyone is fighting their own battles, making choices that suit their circumstances. Some are simply pioneers, charting a path that others will eventually follow. Instead of labelling people, we should seek to understand their journey, as they might just be the trailblazers for a future we haven't yet envisioned.

CHAPTER 9

WOMEN -INFLUENCER IN MY LIFE

Obviously, the most important women in my life have been my mother, my wife, and my two beautiful daughters. I believe this applies to most of us. But there are two other women who made immense contributions to my life.

The first one is my Brahmin Neighbour. No one knew her real name. Everyone called her Mai (mother in Marathi). She was my next-door neighbour, a widow, in the chawl where I grew up in a village near Mumbai.

Although she may not have had a high level of formal education, she was the only woman in our colony who could read and write in Hindi, English & Marathi. Her doors were always open to me, and hers was the only house in the chawl that received newspapers, Diwali magazines, and novels.

She indirectly sparked my interest in reading more and more books and inspired me to study hard. She was overjoyed when I scored 90% on my SSC exams, almost to tears as if her own son had achieved the feat. Unfortunately, I lost touch after we moved to other place and those days, telephones were very rare.

The second one is English Tuition teacher: A formidable woman, Kaku was my English tutor. She charged only INR 5 per month, but her lessons were invaluable. Despite retiring from her regular job, she continued to teach English as a hobby and adding confidence into students like me.

Unlike many teachers, Kaku didn't simply follow a textbook. She emphasised grammar, punctuality, and effective communication. She also shared her personal experiences and taught us about history and English rules. Her English lessons gave me the confidence I needed to succeed in my later years.

These two special women, who were not related to me by blood, had a profound impact on my formative years. I am eternally grateful for their guidance and support. Thank you, Mai and Kaku for shaping my life. I am sure your blessings are always with me.

CHAPTER 10

WAITING ROOM

After scoring around 90% (precisely, 87.42%) in my 10th standard exams, I was advised to pursue engineering. In India back then, the only real choices were to become either an engineer or a doctor.

So, I joined the famous Agarwal Classes in Dadar. For me, it was a daunting task to travel from Karjat every day. I would leave home at 4:30 AM, attend classes, and return by 3:30 PM, only to be met with more assignments.

The biggest challenge, however, was the train schedule. Once my classes ended at 1:00 PM, there was no train to take me home immediately. I would often wait at the railway platform for one or two hours with no other option. Back then, we didn't have mobile phones to pass the time, so I would read books while waiting.

One evening, over dinner, I mentioned to my family how much time I was wasting in the waiting room. My father responded by saying, "These lessons in waiting might help you someday." I was puzzled by his words and didn't quite understand him at the time. I think many young people often don't understand their fathers easily.

But did the habit of waiting patiently ever help me?

I realised later that the stocks or funds I had patiently held in my portfolio for over 10 years provided remarkable returns in terms of CAGR. Also noticed that I waited 5 years to land a good corporate job in reputed EPC, 14 years to earn my first salary in USD from Japanese EPC and 30 years to become a Supply Chain Director.

Now, when I think back to those long afternoons spent at the train station, I no longer see them as wasted time. Those hours, spent immersed in books, helped shape my love for learning and provided the mental calmness needed to handle life's unpredictability. The habit of waiting patiently turned out to be one of the most critical tools in my personal and professional life.

Whether in wealth, career, relationships, or knowledge, life's greatest rewards come through compounded waiting. As with all things, the more time you give, the more the rewards multiply. The lesson my father taught me has stayed with me, a reminder that even in the slowest moments, life is still moving forward, preparing you for the next chapter.

We are all in waiting room – one or other.

CHAPTER 11

ATTENTION SEEKING SYNDROME (ASS)

As a child, I believe I had what could be called an attention-seeking syndrome. It's common in children, though some people never outgrow it, even as they age.

I would always want my mother to wake me up in the morning by cuddling me. She had to come and say goodbye before I left for school and be there to greet me when I returned. Every meal had to be made exactly the way I liked it, and if it wasn't, I'd cry loudly until another family member, usually my grandmother, would step in to resolve the issue.

But once you leave home — first for school and later for the hostel — you begin to realise your true worth, and all these theatrics fade away. However, some people never grow up. They continue to seek attention through various means.

I had a friend in the hostel who admitted he didn't even like smoking, but he did it to gain attention. Similarly, many people seek attention by buying expensive items like iPhones, Rolex watches, BMWs, or Mercedes vehicles, whether they truly need them or not. Brands cleverly position these products as status symbols, so they are often purchased for the image they project rather than their intended function.

In meetings, some people speak up just to get management's attention, even if it means repeating the same points. But you can't entirely blame them—after all, self-promotion is a part of life. Seeking attention based on your work, deeds, and achievements is perfectly fine. However, the moment you rely on products to do so, you may be heading toward self-destruction.

So, check if you have ASS — Attention Seeking Syndrome!

CHAPTER 12

BURDEN OF EXPECTATIONS

As a class topper in school, my parents naturally built-up expectations for me. When I moved to secondary school, my teachers and family also had high hopes. When I transitioned from secondary school to college, there was pressure to top my batch. Then, when I joined an organisation, my boss had high expectations, reminding me that I was chosen after fierce competition and needed to perform.

Once I settled into the organisation, my family expected me to rise through the ranks and earn promotions — if not every year, at least every 2-3 years. There is no limit to what others will expect from you. It's natural for people to have expectations when you're performing well, but the key skill is learning how to manage those expectations.

Life doesn't always go as planned. I became incredibly frustrated by this constant rat race, particularly in the corporate world, especially after I was denied a promotion at a large EPC Company. After reaching a point where I had achieved my set goals, I made a declaration to myself and my family: I was no longer part of this rat race. I just wanted to enjoy my work and earn whatever I deserved.

Most of the time, I was content with my progress. But the moment you start comparing yourself to others from the same batch, in the same organisation, frustration creeps in—especially when family gatherings turn into discussions about promotions and bonuses.

But, life does not stop here. When we become parents, we expect so much from our kids. Why cant someone be only average kid? Why everyone has to become Doctors, Lawyers, Engineers and Charted accounts? Honestly, I have not set any expectations from my kids. Just let them be what they want to . I just want them to be good human being first.

No one desires to become Delivery Agents, taxi driver or receptionist and operator. Our dreams are lost in the struggle of life. But burden of expectation is huge. Don't fall into that trap. Yes, we try our best under all circumstances, we push ourself very hard, we motivate our family to do better but just do Karma. Results must be left to destiny.

How many of us fall into depression because we can't meet someone else's expectations? Why don't we step out of this rat race?

Prioritise your mental health, happiness over anyone else's expectations from you.

CHAPTER 13

KARMA RETURNS

My friend Debojeet called me from Mumbai, seeking financial assistance. I reminded him that he hadn't repaid a previous loan. Despite my reservations, he persistently pleaded for help, citing the needs of his young children. Moved by his emotional appeal, I reluctantly provided some assistance.

Debojeet, the only son of a prominent local businessman, was born into a life of privilege. His father's successful business relied heavily on a network of underpaid and mistreated relatives. Despite widespread knowledge of this situation, no one dared to confront the patriarch.

Years later, the father's deteriorating health led to the business's decline. As employees left to pursue their own ventures, Debojeet, who had never truly appreciated the value of money, found himself increasingly isolated. His parents had failed to instil in him the essential values of humility, kindness, and compassion.

Today, Debojeet, a former diploma engineer, is unemployed and deeply in debt. His lack of support from others can be attributed in part to his own harmful habits, such as chewing paan, masala, and gutkha, and consuming alcohol. With two sons to educate, Debojit's situation has become dire.

As this story demonstrates, unkindness towards others can have far-reaching consequences (Karma). Those who fail to treat others with compassion during times of prosperity may find themselves facing adversity in the future, either personally or through their children. Debojeet's experiences serve as a stark reminder of this principle.

CHAPTER 14

WRONG PRIORITIES – DR KARVE

Dr. Karve and his wife were one of the few educated families in our village/town. Dr. Karve was an MBBS, and Mrs. Karve held a BSc degree. Although they had no immediate blood relatives in the small village, the entire community considered them family due to their kindness and helpfulness.

The couple had two children: a son and a daughter. Both pursued medical school (I believe privately) and higher education in the United States, eventually settling there. The son married an American woman, and the daughter married an Indian-American lawyer. Both children seemed to be living happily.

In the initial years after their marriages, the children visited their parents frequently. However, as their lives became busier, these visits grew less frequent. Once they had children of their own, they almost completely stopped visiting their parents in India. Dr. Karve occasionally traveled to the United States, but he always returned, unable to adjust to the lifestyle there.

As the couple aged and could no longer manage their household chores, they moved to a nursing home. Mrs. Karve passed away during the COVID pandemic. Their children did not attend her funeral due to concerns about the virus. With the help of the villagers, the old doctor was able to conduct the funeral. However, he spent the last three years alone.

Recently, the doctor also passed away. The villagers contacted his children, but they were unable to arrive in time. The villagers once again organised the funeral. While the children may have had their own schedules, neglecting their parents is a significant oversight.

This incident reminded me of Khalil Gibran's poem "Our Children." However, I question the value of such children and families. What is the purpose of education if it leads to such selfishness?

The reality remains:

1. Our children are not our possessions. They will face their own life challenges.
2. Our children are not investments like fixed deposits that guarantee returns.
3. We will likely spend a significant portion of our lives alone, so it's essential to learn to live happily independently.

Fortunately, few children will have such misguided priorities, and we must be prepared for all possibilities.

CHAPTER 15

AN AVERAGE ENGINEER

I am just an average engineer. No high IQ, no stellar GMAT score, and certainly not an IIT or NIT graduate. But here's the surprising part—I'm proud of it. In a world that often celebrates only the exceptional, I represent the 99% who are like me: ordinary people doing extraordinary things in their own ways. Becoming an engineer was, for me, no small feat. It wasn't just a degree; it was a break from tradition and a bold step forward for my family.

I come from a family of traders and small shopkeepers, where no one had ever even graduated before me. So when I earned my engineering degree from K.J. Somaiya College, it was a milestone not just for me but for my entire family. It wasn't about being extraordinary in society's eyes; it was about breaking boundaries and setting a new path for future generations.

But why engineering? It's a question I've often asked myself. Most of my family and friends were in business, making good money. I could have followed that path easily, but something inside me wanted to break away from the familiar. I wanted to forge my own identity, to step outside the box that tradition had placed around me. And that's how I found myself on the path of engineering—a deliberate choice to create something different for myself.

Despite this, I've had my share of struggles. As a mechanical engineer, I've always found complex GA and P&IDs challenging to understand.

Even after 15 years of investing, I still struggle with analyzing balance sheets and cash flow statements. While I hold a certification as a Qualified Personal Finance Professional, I don't always practice what I preach.

Concepts like artificial intelligence and cryptocurrency remain foreign to me, even though I have computer engineers in my family. My professional growth has been steady but far from meteoric, and I've never been the standout performer in any of the organisations I've worked for. In short, I'm an average engineer.

During Covid, I took up writing seriously and started sharing with friends and followers. But social media is double edged sword. It get you addicted and I decided to stop sharing anything with the outside world. I thought nobody will bother about it. No one will care about it.

To my surprise, messages started pouring in from people around the world—especially youngsters and entrepreneurs—telling me how much my words had impacted them. They had been quietly reading my LinkedIn posts, even though they never commented or liked them, finding value in my simple, honest storytelling.

That's when I realised my strength lies in my relatability. I may not have fancy credentials, but I have something just as powerful: the ability to connect with people through real, lived experiences. It's not about grand achievements; it's about being honest and authentic. My journey as an average engineer resonates because it's relatable, and that's what creates impact.

If I can touch the lives of even 1% of my readers, that, to me, is success. I've come to understand that you don't have to be exceptional to make a difference. You just have to be genuine and open.

So here I am, ready to share more of my journey with you—not to impress, but to connect, inspire, and show that even the most ordinary story has the power to change lives.

CHAPTER 16

CAREER – BEGINNING OF LIFE

What is more important in the early stages of your career? Should you focus on learning or earning first? Is the stability of a large corporation better, or should you embrace the uncertainty of a small business or startup?

I recently caught up with a former classmate after a long time. While most of us were busy chasing placements; looking to get hired somewhere, probably anywhere. He had a different approach. He skipped all the campus interviews. His philosophy was simple yet clear: join a small-scale company, learn the ins and outs of product engineering, manufacturing, sales, and marketing. In smaller firms, you can wear many hats and gain exposure to every function.

Those of us who opted for corporate jobs found ourselves confined to specific departments, with structured training programs. But nothing compares to hands-on experience — dealing with real situations and real clients.

Today, my friend owns three small-scale companies, employing around 60 people and generating an annual turnover of INR 50 crore. He has even launched a new software venture, creating additional jobs. Of course, his journey wasn't without its struggles.

Meanwhile, the top students from our batch who joined prestigious corporations are now either hopping from job to job or anxiously awaiting their next promotion—feeling stuck and helpless. Is it destiny? Do you believe in it?

I have the utmost respect for my peers who are creating jobs and supporting families. It's especially important now, in the Post-COVID era.

CHAPTER 17

LUCK BY CHANCE

Some of my school friends, who failed to secure admission into engineering or medical colleges, ventured into their own businesses. Some entered retail, others the transportation business, and a few went into construction. Some even became politicians. After initial struggles, many of them are now earning significant sums in India.

My college mates, who didn't land good jobs with reputed engineering companies during campus placements in the 1990s, turned to APTECH and NEET computer courses. They developed skills in C++ programming, web development, and SAP implementation, and many of them moved to the USA, where they eventually settled.

My office colleagues, who were laid off from reputable EPC companies in India between 2000 and 2003, initially struggled but later moved to the Middle East. They earned millions in petrodollars and now live in palatial villas they could never have afforded had they stayed in their original jobs.

On the other hand, those who were academically bright and secured jobs early on didn't need to take risks. They were content with smaller salaries and never looked beyond the comfort of a stable monthly pay check. Life was easier for them, but their monetary success was limited.

The first three groups had no choice but to take risks and chances — and many succeeded.

What I've learned from this:

- Failure at one stage often opens doors elsewhere. You never know when an opportunity will strike, putting you in the right place at the right time.
- Success at one stage always brings the next level of challenges.
- Those who were initially settled and didn't face many challenges remained stagnant and didn't grow much. Never become complacent, and never stop learning.

Keep trying. Don't let too much analysis lead to paralysis.

CHAPTER 18

GOOD MANAGER – LIFE SHAPERS

I was 22, and he had 44 years of experience. He had retired from the prestigious BARC, India, and joined our project as CEO. I never imagined I would have the chance to meet such a distinguished individual.

Since the team was small in the beginning, during my first week, he called me in. After a brief discussion, he handed me several offers and asked me to prepare bid tabs, which I diligently completed and returned. This soon became a routine. Other team members were puzzled — what was a trainee doing with the CEO?

Once the ordering phase was complete, he assigned me to expedite work with vendors. On one occasion, he sent me to a renowned boiler manufacturing unit, and when I returned, I reported a six-month delay. Our consultant project manager wasn't willing to trust this "new boy," but he did. I had gathered the information directly from the shop floor workers, thanks to my Marathi language skills.

Later, during the commissioning phase, he moved me to the site. On a rainy day, our bus broke down 3 kilometres away from the site. Everyone assumed it was an unplanned holiday, but not him.

He got out, opened his umbrella, and started walking. The rest of us had no choice but to follow.

Thank you, Mr. K. S. Bimbhatt, for being my first mentor in the industry. My key takeaways from you:

- Choose right Manager for your Growth – Just right Company is not sufficient.

- Be the nice Manager to Youngsters. Be a Model for them.

- Believe in Youngsters. They have immense potential. Just give them right opportunity.

Your first manager leaves vast impact on your career and how you will shape up as a Leader. Graduates pick up their habits quickly.

CHAPTER 19

CHANGING GOAL POSTS

CBSE recently declared results for X & XII students, with an impressive 21% scoring 90% and above. This took me down memory lane to when I passed with similar high marks 40 years ago. Back then, I was told:

1. Clear XII: Life will be a dream.

2. Get into engineering: Another milestone.

3. Clear Degree Engineering: Yet another goal achieved.

4. Land the first job Good Company- A new beginning.

5. Earn the first promotion and become Manager: Climbing the ladder.

6. Secure the overseas assignment: Expanding horizons.

Each achievement led to the next goal.

Life, I've realized, is a constant struggle. Whether you're striving to survive, succeed, or find significance, the goalposts keep shifting.

Consider this:

- How many industrialists say, "I made 100 CR, now I'm retiring?" Let someone else make money.

- How many cricket players say, "I made 1000 test runs, now I'm retiring?" Let someone else take my place.

- How many cine stars say, "I gave 3 superhits, now I'm retiring?" Let a new star rise.

Never none.

Everyone struggles. Some for survival, others for success, and many for significance. While the specifics vary, the drive to grow, achieve, and find meaning is universal. Understanding and navigating your own struggles is key to a fulfilling journey.

If you are struggling today, don't worry. Everyone has their share of struggle. Just keep pushing the cart, enjoy the journey, remain true to your values, work hard, and leave the rest to destiny.

CHAPTER 20

ALTERNATE CAREER

Sir Isaac Newton was an English mathematician, physicist, astronomer, theologian, author, philosopher, and one of the most influential scientists of all time. Leonardo da Vinci, an Italian polymath, was active in a multitude of fields including painting, engineering, anatomy, and cartography. Elon Reeve Musk is an entrepreneur and business magnate, the founder, CEO, and Chief Engineer of SpaceX; early-stage investor, CEO, and Product Architect of Tesla, Inc.; founder of The Boring Company; and co-founder of Neuralink and OpenAI. Jeff Bezos, an American entrepreneur, media proprietor, investor, and computer engineer, founded the aerospace manufacturer and sub-orbital spaceflight services company Blue Origin in 2000.

In the film industry, we also see many individuals who are multi-talented — writers, producers, music composers, actors, and singers, all in one person. The question is that — being multi-talented the monopoly of a select few, or is it a reflection of our own unwillingness to develop more skills? Does our education system condition us to master just one art while stifling our ability to grow in others?

- Why can't an Average Engineer be a financial consultant?

- Why can't a Buyer be a singer on weekends or
- Why cant a Software Engineer be a chef on weekends
- Why can't I be Uber Driver in the evening rush hours?

All without conflicts of interest?

Why don't we explore different facets of our talents and develop alternative careers? With the gig economy set to play a major role in the coming years, I believe everyone will need multiple skills — one skill may no longer be enough to thrive.

CHAPTER 21

LOVE OF LOCATION

I spent my childhood and early years of my career in a small town near Mumbai (70 Kms) from Mumbai). I was so much in love with Mumbai during those days that I never ever applied for education or job out of Mumbai.

When I got selected by Large EPC in India and I opted for location of VADODARA – as I was wasting too much time in Train Journey (5 hours a day) but my family resisted. Why move out of Mumbai and go to small town like Vadodara? They felt this decision was influenced my by newly married wife who was from Ahmedabad. I convinced them because of Company brand name.

But, when it came time to leave large Reputed Indian EPC and go to Japan, there was furthermore dilemma. Why do you want to go away from India. We have everything here. But, again I was FIRM on my decision and I want to grow and explore the world. I do not want to restrict my growth because I am in love with some place or some company.

Later, I travelled to USA and now settled for Dubai for last 20 years. When I was shifting my family to UAE my daughter was in 09th std. Everyone was lecturing oh it is so important year and you will spoil her career. But, I was firm. Family has to be with you while you have already spent reasonable time alone making money. Let me tell you, X & XII std results or marks has absolutely no relevance when it comes to higher medical or engg. Admission.

If you want to grow you will have to embrace some discomforts. I have seen many people who do not want to go away from their hometown. Just out of love. Nowadays, girls also look to marry in the same location. No, I want boy only from VADODARA or I want job only in so and so place.

When we limit ourself with location with put wings on our growth.

CHAPTER 22

SLOW DOWN

When I was growing up in India (around 1975), my mother used to cook rice and dal over an earthen chulha using wood and coal. She would leave it to cook and return after two hours, having washed clothes by the nearby lake.

The food cooked through such a slow process was incredibly flavourful and packed with nutrients. When she switched to using a pressure cooker and gas stove in the 1980s, we talked during dinner about how we had sacrificed taste for speed. But my father insisted that we needed to adapt to the changing times.

Eating slowly and chewing mindfully (without distractions from phones or television) has its own benefits. In fact, I've never seen an overweight person who eats very slowly. During my Vipassana workshop, I clearly experienced how slow, deliberate breathing and observing each breath can calm the mind. It brings deep psychological and spiritual benefits.

In metallurgy, heating steel slowly and allowing it to cool at a controlled pace significantly improves its quality. Similarly, hand-crafted gold jewellery, heated and tempered slowly, is far more valuable than machine-made ornaments.

If there are so many benefits to slowing down, why are we in such a rush? Just slow down and saver each moment of life. Warren Buffet began investing at age 11, but most of his wealth came after he turned 60 — a steady, patient process.

Building wealth through equity investment is a similarly slow and sometimes tedious journey, much like the other processes I've mentioned. Would you like to be part of this slow and rewarding path to becoming a millionaire?

CHAPTER 23

HOME COOKED FOOD

My Grandmother used to tell me that she used to cook for a family of 25, almost all the time she is awake -12 hours a day minimum.

I have seen my mother working in the Kitchen, cooking for a family of 10, almost 6-8 hours in a day.

My wife is busy in the kitchen on average 4 hours a day, but she prefers to have day off during the weekend and my daughter, who is working for an IT company, cooks probably during weekends and in between, depending upon schedule.

If you see the sequence, at least in Urban India, time spent in the kitchen is reducing drastically.

Cooking as a daily chore will get eliminated slowly or surely. Cooking will remain only either your hobby or your profession.

The issue is, who will cook? Where are we all going to eat?

Simple, it will be cloud kitchens, restaurants and ready to eat food, giving big flip to the food industry. But the big question here is are they providing healthy and reliable options?

If there is a choice to be made between ETHICS and PROFITS, corporates will always opt for PROFIT.

There are so many products available in the market which are banned in other countries. For example,

The permitted color Auramine – popular blue coloring agent is harmful for liver and kidneys found in various products easily.

Certain dyes like yellow 5, yellow 6 and red 40 are banned in the EU as they are harmful for kids.

Food stabilizer (INS 1450) has an impact on gut health.

Coffee creamer is banned in some countries as it contains trans fats like partially hydrogenated soybean and cottonseed oils.

There is a huge list of products which should be banned but easily available in India.

Better not to talk about Sugary cold drinks and health drinks as there is some awareness amongst people in India. Fast food chains serving food in India are less healthy than their counterparts in the west (high content of trans fat and sodium)

So what are the options: You don't have time to cook at home and outside food is not healthy? Striking a balance between these 2 will be essential.

Technology will play a huge role in doing it. Someone will come up with an app or website where you can hire a home cook, who will come to your home and cook with the ingredients you provided. It will be a huge gig economy providing work to home cooks and comfort to you.

Secondly, few AI based apps will soon come to the market, where they have your health data and you can click pictures of what you are eating and it will provide you details of calories, details of contents – harmful or not, its carbon footprint. – Based on that information you will be able to make an informed decision whether you should have it or not?

Are you cooking at home tonight?

CHAPTER 24

I LOVE DIWALI

This is the only time of the year when I'm allowed to do a deep cleaning of our storeroom and cupboards. We Indians, in general, have a habit of storing everything. Kaam Lagase (it'll be useful). Don't throw it away. Not the old newspapers, magazines, plastic bags, clothes, or even unused electrical equipment. Nothing is allowed to be discarded — because, Kaam Lagase.

Years ago, one shirt would be worn by the elder son, then passed down to the younger one, later turned into a bag, then used to clean an old scooter, and finally thrown into the fire (Chulha). This was the middle-class Indian sustainability cycle. We were one of the most sustainable societies — perhaps not by choice.

Buying is easy. Disposing is hard.

Today, as I looked through our wardrobe, I noticed many clothes that have hardly been worn. Some still have the price tags on them — bought, but never used.

And then there are the special outfits we buy for every cousin's wedding, only to wear them once. These expensive sarees and clothes sit in the closet for years, and when they finally go out of style, we think of donating them to the housemaid. Even she laughs and asks, "Madam, where will I wear this?"

I've made several attempts to sell them second-hand at steep discounts, but none have succeeded. We're so status-conscious — who would wear second-hand clothes?

We've made great economic progress, but in the process, we've forgotten about sustainability. We forget that Mother Earth has limited resources for 8–9 billion people, and we must conserve those precious resources for the next generation.

This is the only gift we can truly give to future generations. What's your plan this Diwali?

I love Diwali.

CHAPTER 25

SCARCITY – A STRATEGY

My phone screen time has decreased by 39% since moving to a new house. Our old single router couldn't reach the balconies or master bedroom, and I haven't installed an additional one, creating a deliberate network shortage. This has worked to my advantage, as other parts of the home have sufficient coverage, ensuring we don't miss any calls or messages.

This led me to consider other examples, such as: My Japanese friend earned approximately 1,200,000 Yen (USD 10,000) per month, but his wife only gave him 30,000 Yen (USD 300 or less) for monthly expenses, primarily cigarettes and drinks. In many Japanese households, the wife manages the finances. He said his wife was very clever, intentionally limiting his spending to reduce waste.

My wealthy Gujju friend in India visits restaurants for good food and drinks (non-alcoholic) weekly but has a strict rule: all payments must be made in cash. Paying with cash can make spending feel more tangible, encouraging him to be more mindful of his expenses. My friend in Mumbai drives an XUV 700 with a 60-litre fuel tank but always fills it with only 55 litres. He believes this saves unnecessary trips.

Scarcity is a strategy used by corporations as well. Consider OPEC's actions to reduce oil supply or the limited-edition ROLEX watches. There are countless examples.

When raising teenagers, you can effectively use this strategy. By providing limited funds, you can teach them the value of money. Similarly, offering limited food options can encourage them to eat nutritious food.

How do you plan to implement this strategy to build wealth or raise your children?

CHAPTER 26

DIFFICULT CONVERSATIONS

One of my cousins is an alcoholic, and his family life is in shambles because of this habit. Everyone knows, but no one wants to confront him or offer advice. A previous boss of mine in India was very eccentric. The whole office was aware of it, yet no one dared to speak to him directly. One of my current colleagues in the UAE has lost his job and wants to return to India, but his wife disagrees. He finds it difficult to initiate the conversation with her and explain that moving back could help them save their dwindling funds and live more affordably.

Difficult conversations are a part of life—whether it's addressing a sensitive issue with a loved one, giving constructive feedback to an employee, or negotiating a business deal. These conversations can be emotionally charged, uncomfortable, and even confrontational, but avoiding them can lead to misunderstandings, resentment, and missed opportunities.

Opening up a difficult conversation is an art. Your ability to persuade plays a crucial role, but most importantly, the person you're speaking to must trust you completely. Building trust and then convincing them takes time. Who has the time for all that? Only your most trusted friends and family members are usually willing to engage in such conversations. To make these discussions productive, it's essential to prepare and approach them with empathy, clarity, and an open mind.

Here are a few tips that can help:

1. **Identify the issue:** Before starting the conversation, be clear about the specific problem you want to address and why it's important.

2. **Choose the right time and place:** Timing and setting are crucial. Pick a time and place where both parties can talk privately and without distractions.

3. **Practice active listening:** Active listening is key in any difficult conversation. Pay attention to the other person's perspective without interrupting, and try to understand their point of view.

4. **Stay calm and respectful:** It's natural to feel emotional, but staying calm and respectful is critical. Avoid accusatory language and focus on the facts rather than personal attacks.

5. **Find common ground:** Look for areas of agreement or shared goals to help find a solution that works for both sides.

6. **End on a positive note:** Even if the issue isn't fully resolved, end on a positive note. Show appreciation for the other person's willingness to engage, and commit to following up and continuing the dialogue.

In conclusion, difficult conversations can be challenging, but they are essential for effective communication and problem-solving. With the right preparation, approach, and mindset, it's possible to navigate these conversations with empathy, clarity, and respect.

CHAPTER 27

YEH DIL MANGE LESS

Before Diwali, it's tradition in Indian households to clean every nook and cranny, ridding our homes of dust and clutter. This year, the task fell to me, and as I started cleaning my room, I was stunned by the sheer volume of things I'd collected over the years—piles of shirts, T-shirts, jeans, shoes, belts, and more. Yet ironically, I'm still labelled as a "kanjoos" — someone who pinches pennies before spending them!

But this is where our minds play tricks on us. The human brain is wired for dissatisfaction, always wanting more. Corporations know this well and exploit it. They flood us with advertisements, convincing us that we need the latest gadgets, trends, and fashions to keep up. Social media has only added fuel to the fire, making it easier than ever to covet what others have.

The other day, I saw a tweet from an investor proudly declaring that Mukesh Ambani, Elon Musk, Tim Cook, and Mark Zuckerberg all work for him. The reality, though, is quite the opposite. We, the consumers, tirelessly use their goods and services — whether we need them or not—while they rake in billions. In truth, we are working for them, not the other way around.

Take a step back and think about it: in the race to pursue the "American Dream" or accumulate more wealth, how often do we pause to consider the impact we're having on the environment or the cruelty inflicted on animals? We chase bigger cars, faster phones, and bigger houses, with little thought to the toll on the planet.

Should reducing our carbon footprint and going green be the sole responsibility of corporations? What about us, the consumers? Shouldn't we also learn to consume only what's necessary?

In the 1990s, Pepsi's slogan was "Yeh Dil Maange More," urging us to crave more of everything. But maybe it's time we reverse that thinking and embrace "Yeh Dil Maange Less!" True happiness doesn't come from having more, but from needing less. By cutting back, staying healthy, and conserving resources, we can ensure a better world for future generations. Let's consume mindfully, because that's the real path to lasting contentment.

CHAPTER 28

BRANDS & ME

Last week, I went to the airport to pick up my daughter. I bought her a beautiful bouquet and dressed up in white Nike shoes, black cargo pants, a green T-shirt, and a stylish black cap to hide my receding hairline.

As soon as she saw me, her first question was about my bulging belly. She asked if I had stopped exercising or was under stress. She completely ignored my outfit.

People who truly care about you will prioritise your health and well-being. Others may focus on your appearance. I blamed it on the recent Diwali festivities, but my real problem is my weakness for Indian sweets and delicacies.

I have all the knowledge and information I need to lose weight, but I'm a complete failure when it comes to discipline. Discipline is destiny, but not when it comes to food.

Is there anyone out there who can help me reduce belly fat while still indulging in my favourite sweets?

CHAPTER 29

SECRET OF FREEDOM

Today, I'm sharing a simple secret to my happiness: I'm not afraid of the "3 Bs"—Bank, Boss, and the final B, which you'll discover as you read on!

1) Bank:

I've stayed debt-free for most of my life. I've never had the stress of EMIs or loans weighing me down. I only use one credit card, and I pay it off in full every month. My spending is always within my income, with savings set aside first. Being financially independent and free from debt is a cornerstone of happiness.

2) Boss:

Many people are intimidated by their bosses, but I believe that just as much as we need a job, the job needs us too. If you work diligently and with integrity, there's no reason to fear any boss. Yes, job loss can happen in rare cases, but when you've built a solid personal brand, honed your skills, and developed a strong network, new opportunities will always come your way.

3) Bairu/Bhaydo/Biwi (Wife):

In Gujarati slang, "Bairu" or "Bhaydo" refers to a spouse—that's the third B. Some married friends live in fear of their wives, making big purchases like bungalows, cars, or jewelry just to avoid saying no. This is ridiculous. Marriage is a partnership, and both partners need to be on the same page about the family's financial goals and budget.

True happiness comes from being free in these three areas. So, how much freedom do you have with the "3 Bs" in your life?

CHAPTER 30

HOUSE OF HAPPINESS

I believe the House of Happiness has 7 pillars!

1. **Paiso (Money)**: Let's face it, folks, money talks and it is a very important part of our life! If you have money 90% of your issues are sorted out - if not all. Those philosophers who say "paisa ni koi kimmat nathi" probably haven't made money any time in life.

2. **Life Partner**: Believe me, having a right life partner is the biggest life hack. The one who can understand you, who's smart, supportive, and you can learn together and grow! Swipe right for happiness!

3. **Health**: You could have all the money in the world and the most amazing partner, but if you're wheezing like a rusty accordion, it's game over, my friend! Remember, your health is your wealth - and no, you can't cash in those six-pack abs at the bank!

4. **Friends & Family**: I love big families. Unfortunately, we have nuclear families now. But, how do you celebrate your success when you have no one to cheer for? Your family cheers you up and provides all the support when you need it. You are an average of 5

persons you are generally surrounded by so having the right family and friends is key to happiness.

5. **Skills & Knowledge:** No one can remove you from job if you have right skills and correct education. It is your own copyright. You can never be dependent if you have right skills. It does not come heriditary. Have unique skills and amplify it with social media.

6. **Country:** I am a proud Indian. It is the one country where you can be rescued from Iran, Yemen or Sudan anywhere. But, there are people around me who have no place to go -if they lose their job. Having a passport from a certain "coveted" country can fast-track your career and change your life. You have no control over it but it has impact on your happiness.

7. Dont ask me for the 7th Pillar. It is you who read my book. You may not like but I love you. You are changing your life.

CHAPTER 31

CONNECTING THE DOTS

In 2002, I was working for a company in Dahej after leaving India's largest EPC company. Despite being passed over for a promotion, I wasn't entirely dissatisfied with my new role. The compensation was decent, but the location was remote, and the constant travel was physically and mentally exhausting. I had left behind the comfort of familiar surroundings—friends, family, leisurely afternoon lunches, and a regular schedule that allowed me to be home by 7 PM. But I made this move to prove something—not just to those at a large EPC Company but also to myself and my family.

After about a year at Dahej, a completely unexpected opportunity came my way. A company in Japan approached me, and after going through written exams and a telephonic interview, I received an offer to join them. At that moment, I had never travelled beyond Mumbai, let alone to another country. It was my first international flight, and I had two young kids. Most people would have hesitated, weighed the pros and cons, or waited for the "perfect" moment to make such a big decision. But I didn't overthink it. I simply took the plunge.

That decision changed everything. I earned a substantial income, saved enough to buy my first house, and eventually travelled to places I had only dreamt of, including the USA and the Middle East. Over time, I accumulated not just financial wealth but invaluable life experiences. In hindsight, it may seem like I had a clear vision and knew exactly what I was doing, but the truth is, I didn't. I was navigating uncharted waters with no roadmap, no guarantees, and no certainty about the future.

What I've learned from that experience is that waiting for the "right moment" can often mean waiting forever. The truth is, the perfect moment rarely exists. The key to success lies in making decisions and committing to making them right. Often, we hesitate, waiting for clarity or ideal conditions, but in doing so, we miss opportunities that could change our lives.

I believe it's okay to feel lost and unsure because that's how every meaningful journey begins. Success doesn't come from waiting for the right time—it comes from making bold decisions, taking action, and learning to adapt along the way. Only in hindsight do we see the clarity and sense behind the choices we made.

CHAPTER 32

BOOKS THAT SHAPED ME

I try to read as many books as possible in my free time. Books in India are much cheaper compared to those available here, so during my trips to India, a visit to Crossword is a must. Some books have had a life-changing impact on me, and the following are the ones that have influenced my life the most.

- **7 Habits of Highly Effective People – By Stephen Covey**
  My Company organised a one-day training program on 7 Habits, which was beautifully explained by the instructor. It was my first introduction to the concept of a paradigm shift and the idea of focusing on your circle of influence rather than complaining about things beyond your control. This book became a reference guide for me, especially during times when I faced challenges in my job or personal relationships.

- **Water & You – Dr. Mantena Satyanarayana Raju**
  This book was life-changing, not just for me but for my entire family. I finished it in one sitting, right at the airport. It was so simple and convincing that I began following its advice the very next day, with amazing results. One day, I left the book on the table, and my wife picked it up and started reading. It transformed our family's lifestyle, and everyone began drinking

plenty of water every morning. It helped prevent many potential lifestyle diseases.

- **My Experiments with Truth – Mohandas Karamchand Gandhi**
Not everyone is fond of Mohandas Karamchand Gandhi, even in India, but I read his autobiography first in Gujarati and later in English. I believe everyone has their strengths and weaknesses, but we should focus on the positives. The honesty with which this book is written is beyond anything I could have imagined. It reinforced why truth and non-violence are such powerful forces. After reading it, I never doubted their importance again.

- **The Secret – Rhonda Byrne**

I didn't believe in the power of positive thinking until I experienced it myself. I was carrying this book on the day of my final driving test. Those who have taken the UAE driving test know how significant this milestone is. Throughout the day, I kept thinking I would pass on my first attempt, and I did! Whether it was a coincidence or not, it made a huge impact on me.

- **The Almanack of Naval Ravikant – A Guide to Wealth and Happiness**
This is an incredible book for anyone looking to build health, wealth, and long-lasting happiness. After reading it, I stopped consuming sugar and started taking cold water baths. The impact on both my health and happiness has been immense.

I'm a slow learner. During my first reading of a book, I try to gauge whether it's good enough for me. If it is, I re-read it multiple times to fully grasp its lessons. I also love the smell of books, so I prefer physical copies over reading on Kindle.

- **Bhagavad Gita**

I haven't fully read or understood this book yet. I've tried many times, but its true meaning is hard to grasp. Every version written by different authors offers unique perspectives, but the core principle remains the same: believe in karma, and leave the rest to God.

CHAPTER 33

ECOSYSTEM

As we prepared for a 2-3 week trip to India, I moved my outdoor plants indoors, away from hot summer environment to cooler in-house environment, placing them near a window to ensure they still received sunlight. Upon our return, I was pleasantly surprised to see the plants flourishing, blooming in ways I hadn't expected. The plants themselves hadn't changed, yet their environment made a significant difference in their growth. This realisation reminded me of how crucial our surroundings are—not just for plants, but for humans as well.

This concept applies to all aspects of life. I've often reflected on why some NRIs (Non-Resident Indians), who maintain strict discipline abroad, behave differently when they return to India. For example, during my trip, a friend who had been highly disciplined while living in Dubai immediately reverted to old habits upon landing in India. He began chewing tobacco (mawa/gutka) and spitting on the streets, something that would have been unthinkable in Dubai. His habits didn't change, but the environment influenced his behaviour.

The same holds true in professional settings. Often, we stagnate in one job, not due to lack of ability but because of the limitations of our environment. I recall a former colleague who left our company a few years ago. Initially, his growth had plateaued, but after switching jobs, he thrived and is now a department head at a major multinational corporation. His growth wasn't about changing who he was; it was about finding the right environment that nurtured his potential.

We often hear the saying that we are the average of the five people we spend the most time with. This is a reflection of how much our surroundings, or ecosystem, influence our behavior and personal development. It's vital to assess whether the environment we are immersed in encourages our growth or stifles it. Are we surrounded by people who uplift and challenge us to become better? Just like plants need the right light and space to thrive, we too need environments that foster our growth, both personally and professionally.

CHAPTER 34

FAILURE – LESSONS IN LIFE

Around 90% of startups fail. Similarly, 99% of IIT aspirants don't make it, and the same goes for NEET and CA exams. In trading, 95% of traders don't turn a profit, with only 1-2% truly making good money. The examples of failure are countless.

But are these challenges unique to exams or business alone? Let's look at nature and its laws:

- How many seeds actually grow into trees?
- How many eggs and sperms successfully result in life?
- How much of the rain falls on land versus what is lost over the sea?

Failure is a universal experience. I, have faced countless failures. In exams, career & investment. It's frustrating, even disheartening at times. However, the key is to never let failure define or overshadow you. These experiences—whether in exams, careers, or life—teach you one important lesson: how to handle failure. You won't always succeed in everything—be it your career, relationships, or business. But every failure brings with it a valuable lesson.

Failure isn't the opposite of success; it's a stepping stone toward it. A degree earned after seven years instead of four is still a degree. A BMW at 60 instead of 30 is still a BMW. Whether you pass your UAE driving test on the first try or after three attempts, the license remains the same.

My daughters, who are otherwise very studious and successful, when they failed in Driving Tests in UAE, I was happy. If we don't allow our kids to fail anytime and help them to pass over every difficulty in life, it is not a good sign. Let your children experience failure so when they don't get promoted in their adulthood they don't get into depression.

Always think that you are just a step away from final destination.

CHAPTER 35

RISK – TAKE IT ON

I believe taking risks early in life is far more beneficial. If you succeed, you gain name, fame, and wealth. If you fail, the lessons learned can guide you later on.

I joined a large EPC Company in 1995 with the intention of retiring from this respected company. Unfortunately, their power plant projects never materialised. When they began downsizing, I chose to leave in 2002 after not being promoted.

I took a **Risk** and joined Hindalco in Dahej, 180 km away from home, friends, and family. I could only see my family once a week. It was a decision made by my heart, not my head, as I felt humiliated at a large EPC Company.

A year later, I was interviewed and selected by IHI, Japan. Once again, I decided to take a risk. Having never been out of India and being a strict vegetarian, the challenge was significant. Leaving behind my two young daughters and family was a risky decision. But, as before, it was a decision made by my heart, not my brain. Had I known about SWOT analysis back then, I might have chosen a different path.

Working for IHI in Japan provided substantial monthly savings, and I stayed there for almost three years, achieving financial independence due to high savings and low expenses. Since then, it's been 20 years working outside India. Along the way, I built a strong investment portfolio to protect my family from potential income loss.

I could now pretend that I had a clear vision, goals, and plans, but the truth is, I had no clue in either case. And that's okay. It's perfectly fine to be clueless and take risks when you're young. The moment you start consulting 10 different people, it means you're not ready to take that risk.

Are you ready to take a **Blind Risk?**

CHAPTER 36

RAT RACE

In 2003, I made the decision to resign from my job at India's largest EPC company. Despite my best efforts and consistent performance, it became clear that I wasn't part of their long-term plans. I wasn't promoted, nor was I identified as a key resource. While this was their decision, I knew I had given my all and believed I had done my best.

Working in a small town or company comes with its own set of challenges, one of the biggest being the close-knit community where everyone seems to know everything about your life. The constant comparisons were exhausting. Even in social circles, especially among the women, discussions often centred on their husbands' promotions and pay raises. It was frustrating to hear, "Your husband didn't get promoted?" repeatedly. The weight of these conversations was stifling, making it hard to focus on anything but external validation.

So, I decided to leave them. Tried my luck abroad, where I was able to earn my first million in INR, buy a house, purchase a car, and settle my family. I told my family, "This is it. Don't expect me to chase after promotions or run in any more rat races. I want to grow at my own pace." Honestly, I believe they trusted me.

Opting out of the traditional race for success didn't mean I became complacent. Many people think that if you're not competing with others, you're not growing. I disagree. I firmly believe in competition, but not with others—my competition is with myself. Each year, I aim to outperform the person I was the year before. I have goals, plans and actions planned for every year and those are monitored by my personal development coach.

One of the things I learned early on is that in society, financial success is often the only metric people use to define you. Other achievements don't seem to matter. That realisation led me to immerse myself in the world of investment and finance. I began reading at least a dozen books each year on the subject, and I soon understood the power of compounding and long-term financial planning.

Today, I am a full-time investor, writer, speaker, and, of course, a supply chain professional. I've stepped out of the race for meaningless competition. My only competitor now is myself — every single day. Just improve bit by bit and inch by inch every day.

CHAPTER 37

TIME AND PATIENCE

For a long time in my career, I've relied on patience as one of my key negotiation tools. I never showed eagerness to close a deal at any cost, even when I was under pressure to do so—whether it was buying furniture for my home or turbines for a power plant.

However, with increasing pressure on schedules, buyers are often under so much strain that they can no longer afford the luxury of patience in negotiations. During my recent trip to India, I needed to install pigeon nets across all my balconies, so I contacted three vendors (following the basics of procurement), asking them to take measurements and provide estimates.

One vendor came immediately and quoted INR 30 per square foot. He clearly sensed our urgency after my wife mentioned that we'd be leaving the following week. Later that evening, another vendor showed up and quoted INR 20 per square foot, unaware of our time constraints. I told him we'd get back to him.

While traveling to Ahmedabad, I casually browsed classifieds and found the same brand and product for INR 10 per square foot! The moral of the story? If you have time and patience, you can negotiate effectively and stay within budget.

These days, everything feels urgent. No project team wants to wait, and no client wants to delay. This sense of urgency often leads us to pay a higher price. Even when I ask vendors to submit prices within 3 days, they provide one quote. But if I ask them to take 30 days, they give a different, often better, price.

Elon Musk once said, "If you give 30 days to do a 3-day task, the work will expand to fill the time." But I disagree with him. Not everyone is Musk. Most of us are ordinary human beings, and we need time.

Time is of the essence, and patience is a virtue!

CHAPTER 38

DANDHO – ENTREPRENEURSHIP

I think entrepreneurs are slightly crazy people. Even though we had very small shop I have seen struggle which my father used to go through. In those days, you could not do business without giving credit to even small consumers in the village. You may or may not get money and there is constant struggle to keep yourself up against those Marwari shopkeepers who used to have deep pockets.

In 1999-2000, My brother established Real Estate Consultancy company in Vadodara and after lots of struggle we were able to close 2-3 deals. Suddenly, earthquake happened in everything collapsed.

Building a business can take 3 to 5 years out of your life. Long, hard days where you remain focused on only one thing. Customers, Consumers, Cash and Competition. The probability of being a successful business, according to some research data, is less than 10 % and **90% of startups** & Businesses **fail** due to one reason or another.

So, you see, it is quite logical why only delusional people build startups. But you and I need these crazy entrepreneurs. How else would we have all these products we didn't know we so needed and now can't give up?

But seriously, startups are expected to drive India's growth to become a $5 trillion economy.

Let there be many more unicorns and rainbows in our life. As and When I return to India, my goal is to support micro-businesses—grocery stores, bakeries, florists, small eateries, laundromats, and spas. I want to help them grow, create jobs, and contribute to local communities.

Creating jobs should not be limited to few select industrialists. All of us can be entrepreneur. Gujarati's have best mind when it come to Dandha.

Be a Entrepreneur. Create Value, Create Jobs.

CHAPTER 39

SUNNY SIDE UP

Just finished taking down all the Diwali decorations and lights. In the Middle East, houses are spacious, but electrical sockets aren't conveniently placed in every corner, so you end up running cables and extension boards everywhere. From the outside, the lights look beautiful — dancing, colourful but behind the scenes, it's a mess of tangled wires and overlapping tapes. It's a bit of a chaotic affair.

We often focus on showcasing the best parts of our lives, whether on social media or elsewhere. The struggles we face in our jobs, relationships, and careers remain for us to deal with alone. Even when people could help, they often don't, and sometimes no amount of money or status can ease the pain our loved ones go through. Everyone faces the consequences of their own Karma.

At the same time, sharing your hardships with others can often lead to them taking a kind of sadistic pleasure in your misfortune. That's why, in difficult times, having truly good friends and supportive family members who stand by you no matter your circumstances, whether you're wealthy or not, employed or not becomes essential.

I've many colleagues, friends, and followers, to who I show my Sunny Side but my real strength is my family and my close relatives with whom I can share my difficulties without being jusdged.

Who is your Support System?

CHAPTER 40

REGRETS IN LIFE

"What are your regrets in life?" my coach asked. "I have no regrets," I replied. "Are you sure?" he reiterated. "If you have no regrets, it means you have not failed enough." His argument put me on the defensive. "Think it over. If you have regrets, write them down."

Here are my top three regrets:

1. **Professional:** I believe I am capable of much more than my current role. However, I have not been sufficiently proactive. I always thought I could handle independent projects or even lead a small company. I could be responsible for the profitability of independent projects or products, but I have not taken the initiative. I was content with my salary and benefits and never approached my department to express my desire for a more challenging role. Unless you ask, no one offers opportunities. I knew that Supply Chain had limitations in terms of growth, but I was complacent.

2. **Personal:** I have few childhood friends. All my current friends are colleagues. Unlike childhood friends who are fiercely loyal, I lack that deep connection. My family is

also small, making it difficult to organise large gatherings or get-togethers. I feel somewhat friendless. Many in my family believe I am overly self-focused and tire of my constant advice. So, I stopped offering unsolicited guidance. They are right.

3. **Physical:** I never played any active sports. The joy and exercise derived from sports are unparalleled. However, due to my academic focus, I neglected building muscle or the strength required for active sports. I played some casual street cricket, but nothing beyond that.

So, can I say I have no regrets? All those regrets were due to certain circumstances, but I have addressed them. Rather than dwelling on regrets, I have found ways to cope with them.

CHAPTER 41

GRATITUDE – EXPRESS IT

The other day, my daughter wrote to me from the USA, thanking me for the wonderful life I've given her so far. I replied that it's simply my duty as a parent. She responded, "It's also my duty to express my gratitude to you as often as I can — it costs nothing."

This sparked a chain reaction in my mind. I thought, why not express my gratitude to all the people who've helped shape my life? Why do we often reserve our kind words for people only at their last rites, in obituaries, or during memorial services?

I made a list of people who've had a significant impact on my life. I sent them heartfelt WhatsApp messages, explaining how they had helped me. Believe me, it created a ripple of positivity. Out of the 10 people I reached out to, 8 were friends and colleagues, and only 2 were relatives.

Coincidentally, the very next day, I read an article in the Khaleej Times about the benefits of expressing gratitude. It highlighted how it strengthens relationships, positively impacts mental well-being, cultivates empathy and kindness, fosters positivity, and enhances self-awareness and personal growth.

So, express your gratitude to those who've helped you along the way. Gratitude can truly transform your attitude. Who knew I would learn such a valuable lesson from a child?

In my 30 years of career, I have helped not less than 50+ candidates to get proper job by providing my reference or providing interview opportunities or some way or other I have helped people. But, did any one express Gratitude? I am yet to experience it.

CHAPTER 42

POWER OF GIVING

I have a strong mindset of accumulating wealth. Honestly, I'm not naturally inclined to spend money, whether for professional or personal reasons. In the past, even when I had the option to fly business class or stay in five-star hotels, I rarely took advantage of these luxuries. While this had some negative consequences, those are a topic for another discussion.

Given my decades-long focus on accumulating wealth, I still find it challenging to loosen my purse strings. However, over time, my perspective has shifted slightly, and my family has consistently encouraged me to engage in charitable activities that don't necessarily lead to more money or material possessions.

On my mother's first death anniversary, we decided to visit a local fishing community and distribute essential goods, including food and other useful items. We were overwhelmed by the number of people in need, and their faces lit up with gratitude as we offered our assistance. Witnessing their joy was incredibly rewarding.

My personal experience that day was truly transformative. Acts of kindness have a profound impact on our mood and bring immense positivity into our lives. They help us feel useful and purposeful, fostering a strong sense of community.

Even small gestures, such as helping a car cleaner, a food court worker, or a toilet cleaner, can go a long way in cultivating kindness within yourself.

Believe in the Power of Giving!

CHAPTER 43

COMMON SENSE

Just happened to meet my Dhobi (Laundryman), after a long time, 06 months- in the Building Elevator.

Thought to myself, his Business must be down — who is calling for Laundry Service while everyone is working in T Shirt & Bermuda?

As a courtesy, casually asked him, how is the business? Bahut Accha (very good), came reply back. I was shocked and surprised?

Looking at my expressions, he himself explained Hospital and Pharma staff are now calling me daily. Same with Police and other uniformed staff of department stores, airports etc. Moreover, many small shops closed. I am doing good.

With hospital connections, I am thinking to start Hospital Waste Disposal Services (HWDS).

Who says right strategy, diversification is required only for oil & gas business? It is required everywhere, and we call it common sense.

(INSERT PICTURE) – A Laundry man with big smile on his face in Elevator

CHAPTER 44

SHAPE IN OR SHIP OUT

I once used a now-infamous phrase for a team member who struggled to meet even the most basic expectations: either you're part of the team, or you walk out. This individual consistently failed to show up on time for meetings or the office, ignored established procedures, and neglected the team's weekly goals.

Diversity of thought is always welcome in any team, but you can't walk into every meeting with objections and arguments. We're not working on cutting-edge product development or complex research that demands constant debate. Our focus is on executing projects that, while important, are fairly straightforward.

Success here is driven by flawless execution, not boundless creativity. In my view, if someone has difficulty fitting into the team's rhythm and structure, they should either make a sincere effort to adapt or move on. It doesn't mean they need to leave the organisation altogether, but perhaps they should seek a different team where their approach may be a better fit.

I've met many professionals earning handsome salaries who still resist every management decision, dragging the team down with their constant pushback. At some point, it's about choice: either SHAPE IN—align with the direction and contribute—or SHIP

OUT—find another role where you can thrive. It's simple. You're either in or out. There's no in-between.

However, this does not apply to your family set up. There is no shipping out. You manage with every one who is part of family. Family is the place where we co-operate and we manage to adjust which each other. As no one is perfect – we just learn from each other and move ahead with life.

Companies who say they are family are big liars. Business is business and family is family. You do not throw out anyone from family if you are not making enough money.

CHAPTER 45

HUMAN TOUCH

For the last 10 years, I have been visiting the nearby Carrefour every weekend, yet I don't know anyone there, and they don't know me either.

For the last 5 years, I've been purchasing a book every month from Amazon, but still, I don't know anyone at Amazon, nor do they know me.

The same goes for my bank and many other retailers. There is a complete loss of human connection, particularly in consumer-facing or retail businesses.

Fortunately, in my profession of Procurement, we must engage with the sellers. We have to call them, listen to them, and build trust with them. We address their concerns and solve their challenges.

It requires a lot of effort and human interaction! Only after doing all this, sometimes, can we strike a deal that meets the target price and schedule.

Hopefully, computers and robots won't be able to replace this part of my job. And who ever said procurement is a boring, mechanical post-office job? You just need to raise the bar.

Stay happy, healthy, and keep interacting — with a human touch.

CHAPTER 46

INDIVIDUAL GOALS

A relative of mine who was 73 years old and had a heart condition required constant medication for blood pressure and blood thinners. Due to issues with urine flow, he consulted a urologist who recommended surgery for prostate enlargement.

Following the surgery, the patient experienced persistent bleeding, and the cardiologist was hesitant to risk stopping the blood-thinning medication. Despite consultations between the cardiologist and urologist, neither was willing to deviate from their established protocols, focusing solely on individual performance metrics. Tragically, the patient passed away.

This is not a fictional story but a real-life example of the need for a holistic approach to healthcare, where the patient's overall well-being takes precedence. Neither a healthy heart nor a healthy prostate is sufficient on its own; both must function in harmony.

Does this principle apply to corporate life as well? If Sales, Marketing, Proposal, Procurement, and Quality each prioritise individual goals, how will the company's overall profitability be affected?

What will happen to corporate growth, reputation, and long-term survival? Can these factors be solely left to the CEO or managing director?

Are you the one looking at the bigger picture?

CHAPTER 47

RESPONSIBILITY & RECOGNITION

Since the lockdown and WFH began, making early morning masala chai has become part of my daily routine. Applying my well-honed corporate practices, I've standardised the entire process — precisely measured quantities of water, milk, tea, sugar, and specific brands. The only variable I leave open is the ginger.

Once the tea is brewed and strained, I place it on the table and wait for my wife's feedback. If there's no comment, it means the performance is good. But occasionally, she'll say, "What on earth have you made? You must've been checking your phone while preparing it."

"Honey, the whole process is standardised," I reply, "and the only variable is the ginger — which you bought. You always have a habit of blaming me." The quick retort? "You always find an excuse!"

It's not too different from the situations we many of us face at our corporate offices.

As a Parents, if you decide when your child has to play, when he has to study, when he will go for classes which classes than you should take responsibility for all outcome. Fortunately, my parents never interfered. I was left to do my own plan.

In a Corporate world if we follow all systems, procedures, guidelines and still do not achieve desired sales target who is responsible? Who takes the blame?

CHAPTER 48

PATIENCE

I believe patience is one of the key virtues when it comes to negotiations, especially tough ones. If you repeatedly call the vendor for final prices and conclusions, you're unlikely to get the best deal because they'll sense your urgency.

However, with tighter project schedules, buyers often have no choice but to push suppliers to expedite. Moreover, negotiations are usually won by the party that cares less about the outcome.

This applies to personal life as well. 99% of the time, I end up apologising to my spouse because she embodies both of these great virtues: patience and a "who cares?" attitude. I'm sure many of us can relate.

Patience isn't just essential for negotiations; it's crucial in many areas, like building your portfolio, acquiring new skills, or even wooing your significant other. Everything takes time.

Yet, in this fast-paced world, patience and focus have become victims of time. After completing a Vipassana course, I challenged myself to meditate for 45 minutes daily for 45 consecutive days — just closing my eyes and focusing on my breath. I failed miserably, managing only 3 out of 45 days. No patience, no focus.

Do you have patience? What's your score? Try it out. Our only competition is with our own thoughts, not with anyone else.

CHAPTER 49

ETHICS AT THE HEART

A purchase order was placed with a sculptor to create a statue that was to be installed on a 40-foot-high pedestal. When the buyer visited for inspection, he was surprised to find two identical statues.

"Why are there two? I only ordered one," the buyer remarked. The sculptor replied, "You will only take one — whichever you prefer." After a thorough inspection, the buyer couldn't find any flaws in either of the statues. Curious, he asked the sculptor for the real reason behind making two.

The sculptor pointed to the nose of one statue and said, "There's a slight chip here." The buyer responded, "Oh no! But who's going to notice it from 40 feet up?"

"I know no one will see it," the sculptor said, "but I will sign this piece, and I know it's there." We had a similar experience with a Japanese supplier who refused to dispatch material even after a successful inspection. When I visited their facility, they explained that they had used SS 316 instead of SS 316L for some internal parts.

It was technically acceptable, but they insisted on replacing the parts and later air-freighted the corrected materials at their own expense. Their reasoning? "Our family name is on this equipment."

Ethics is about doing the right thing, even when no one is watching. It's called integrity, character, or something similar, but it's incredibly difficult to assess during interviews or tender evaluations.

Unfortunately, it rarely makes it onto the evaluation table. How much importance do you give to brand reputation when making purchasing decisions for your organisation?

And more importantly, are you meticulously building your own personal brand?

CHAPTER 50

BOSS IS ALWAYS RIGHT?

Have you ever prepared a Purchase Order (PO) just because your boss asked you to? As a Junior Executive, my boss, Mr. Somani (name unchanged), once asked me to prepare a PO for INR 1 lakh in 1994 for the supply of flowers to the office. However, I refused, stating, "I'm an engineer, not here to buy flowers." He was shocked by my bluntness, but I felt I hadn't done anything wrong.

At that time, I knew nothing about compliance, procedures, or audits. What guided me was the simple principle instilled in me from my upbringing: **Khotu Kaam Karavu Nahi** (Don't engage in anything unethical). If something doesn't feel right, ask questions. If you're still uncomfortable, say no.

Later, I found out that the order was a bribe, placed with the company owned by a government official's wife. Thank God, I hadn't been part of that corruption. Privately, Mr. Somani appreciated my integrity. While Supply Chain Management (SCM) is a support function, I've always believed we should serve our internal customers as efficiently as possible. But blindly following orders can have serious consequences. As the initiator of the PO, the responsibility to justify the order during an audit or vigilance check would ultimately fall on you.

Today, there's much more awareness among buyers about procedures, compliance, vigilance, and audits. If you're not convinced, don't proceed. Still, some buyers fall prey to unethical practices. Be a responsible employee under all roles. Ethics and compliance should be at the core of everything we do.

And other day, Mr. Raghuveer called me back to office at 7.00 PM. I have just reached home and he wanted me to be in office to review presentations which I have provided him at 2 PM. I was junior engineer but I refused to go back to office. He was shocked by my reaction and I was equally shocked that how I had courage to refuse him while I was not financially independent also? But I had done my work. Next day morning he reviewed with me and thanked me for wonderful presentation.

Work hard, work with all honesty and sincerity. It is not necessary that Boss is always right.

CHAPTER 51

DIFFERENT PERSPECTIVE

My wife, according to my in-laws, is considered a better driver than I am on UAE roads. However, whenever I'm in the passenger seat, I can't help but feel anxious. I find myself frequently pointing out her speed, sharp braking, or how closely she drives to other vehicles. But I've realised it's less about her driving and more about me being used to my own style when I'm behind the wheel.

A close friend of mine, who transitioned from being an actor to a director, once shared that he believes there are no good actors left in the industry. His viewpoint shifted entirely once he moved behind the camera, seeing the craft through the lens of a director.

Similarly, when a CFO steps into the CEO role, they might feel that the finance department is poorly managed. Their broader responsibility changes their perspective on how things should function.

Anytime you're exposed to a different vantage point, whether it's in personal or professional life, it can be unsettling. You start questioning and critiquing things that once seemed fine from your familiar position.

This reminds me of when my father used to comment on how I manage finances. He had always been in charge of handling money in our household, and when I took over, he was sceptical of my decisions, even though I followed a different yet effective approach. It took him time to adjust to my way of doing things.

Whenever you move from one role or perspective to another, it can be uncomfortable, and you naturally question things that you weren't responsible for before.

This happens in organisations, too, where senior members often criticise management without understanding the broader picture. I believe leaders should be given the benefit of the doubt, as they have a different and often more comprehensive perspective. Constant criticism from those who don't see the full picture can be detrimental.

I always believed that rotation of the job roles is key in the organisation. People will have to understand each other's role & view. Like start taking care of kids and cooking during weekend and you will realise how hard it is to manage household?

CHAPTER 52

TRUST – EARN IT

Charles **Boldin**, a renowned daredevil tightrope walker, immigrated from France to the United States. In 1858, he achieved a remarkable feat by crossing Niagara Falls on a slender hemp rope, a mere two inches in diameter and 1,300 feet long. This precarious crossing, with the roaring waters below, captivated a massive crowd of 25,000 spectators, including journalists, judges, congressmen, and lawyers.

Boldin's daring acts continued to amaze audiences, as he performed his tightrope walks blindfolded and with increasing levels of difficulty. To further elevate the stakes, he one day proposed a challenge to the crowd: someone could join him on his tightrope, sitting on his arms.

However, despite Boldin's impressive track record and credibility, no one in the crowd was willing to risk their life for such a daring endeavour.

The incident highlights a crucial aspect of trust: **people are more likely to entrust their lives or finances to individuals with whom they have a personal connection or a history of positive interactions.**

Just as we choose doctors based on trust and personal recommendations rather than solely on their credentials or the size of their hospital, we apply similar criteria to other professional services. While online shopping has become commonplace, professional services like those provided by doctors, lawyers, financial advisors, and coaches often require a personal relationship and trust to be effective.

Trust

$$T_{\text{Trustworthiness}} = \frac{C_{\text{redibility}} + R_{\text{eliability}} + I_{\text{ntimacy}}}{S_{\text{elf-Orientation}}}$$

If you want to be a successful professional, start by building trusting relationships with people. In my opinion, relying solely on emails, LinkedIn connections, and MS Teams meetings won't get you far. COVID is over, the masks are off, and it's time to re-establish face-to-face relationships and connections. It will take time and efforts to build trust. It is not easy. It takes time to build and gets destroyed with one simple incidence.

CHAPTER 53

CATALYST - FIND THEM

In chemistry, catalysts speed up reactions without being consumed, making processes more efficient. In life, certain individuals act as catalysts, accelerating our personal and professional growth without depleting their own resources. These people can play a pivotal role in helping us reach our goals faster, just as a catalyst does in a chemical process.

In industries like oil and gas, catalysts are critical for processes such as refining, reducing energy consumption, and increasing output. Similarly, in our lives, the right mentors, collaborators, or friends can significantly enhance our progress. Their guidance, motivation, and influence can act as powerful accelerators for success.

One such example is the partnership between **Narayana Murthy** and **Nandan Nilekani** at Infosys. Narayana Murthy founded Infosys, but it was the leadership team, including Nilekani, who helped scale the company into a global IT giant. Nilekani was pivotal in driving Infosys's global delivery model, which revolutionised the outsourcing industry. Murthy's vision and Nilekani's execution acted as catalysts for each other, propelling Infosys to international success

Another example is Dr. A.P.J. Abdul Kalam, often regarded as the "Missile Man" of India, who credited his early mentor, Dr. Vikram Sarabhai, with shaping his career. Dr. Sarabhai's vision and mentorship accelerated Kalam's growth in space and missile technology, enabling him to make groundbreaking contributions to India's defence and space programs. Sarabhai was the catalyst in Kalam's journey, pushing him to dream big and work toward the nation's development.

Even in the arts, legendary music composer A.R. Rahman had his life-changing moment when Mani Ratnam gave him a chance to score for Roja. Ratnam acted as a catalyst, introducing Rahman's genius to the world, which revolutionised Indian film music.

Life's catalysts often appear through personal or professional networks, influencing and propelling us forward. By staying open to new connections, you allow the right catalysts to help you achieve your potential, just as in chemical reactions.

Find out people who will work as catalyst in your life. People who can propel your career. They may be in around you – in your office, in your house or within friend circles or college.

CHAPTER 54

ZEROSUM GAME

Business has become a Zero-Sum Game. In a Zero-Sum Game, one party's gain necessitates another's loss. This is akin to sports or elections, where only one side emerges victorious. However, this philosophy is incompatible with the nature of business. Ideally, all parties involved should benefit, with profits shared rather than contested.

Unfortunately, today's business landscape often deviates from this ideal. Many large companies have established reputations that deter collaboration. EPCs, vendors, sub-vendors, and traders may be reluctant to work with certain entities due to perceived unfair practices or a lack of mutual benefit.

To address this issue, businesses with substantial financial resources must adopt a more compassionate approach. Instead of being driven solely by legal and financial considerations, they should embrace a leadership philosophy that prioritises collaboration and mutual growth.

A true leader understands that success is not achieved by dominating others but by empowering them. By creating an environment where everyone can thrive, a leader inspires loyalty, trust, and ultimately, greater collective achievement.

For me, life is not a Zero-Sum Game. I believe in fostering win-win situations, even if it means sacrificing short-term financial gains. By investing in the success of others, I create a more sustainable and fulfilling business ecosystem.

CHAPTER 55

DISCIPLINE IS THE DESTINY

I attribute all my success to highest level of Discipline. I am very particular about time. Slightest delay is not acceptable to me.

Discipline should be a core value for all organisations, not just a principle limited to military life. In today's world of flexible hours and remote work, maintaining organisational discipline has become increasingly challenging.

Discipline is a key to success in all aspects of life. While many believe they can achieve greatness without following rules, numerous examples from sports, entertainment, and beyond reveal the pitfalls of unchecked indulgence. Countless iconic figures — athletes, singers, and actors — have fallen into the trap of addiction or self-destruction, often driven by the temptations of wealth and fame.

When you have the power to acquire anything, self-discipline becomes your safeguard against downfall. With easy money you can buy Alcohol. Cigarettes, Drugs, Sugar & Junk food which will destroy you physically and mentally. Yet, in today's culture, discipline is often dismissed or even scorned. Many people take pride in their financial success, despite lacking self-control, but I believe unchecked indulgence in short-term pleasures inevitably leads to long-term suffering.

To cultivate good habits and avoid bad ones, we must be intentional. This means creating an environment that minimises temptation, surrounding ourselves with positive influences, and consistently practicing self-discipline. While discipline may not be popular, it is critical for sustained success. There's nothing commendable about living a disorganised life.

Every achievement involves some measure of sacrifice. A bit of pain and discipline is not a roadblock to success; rather, it is a steppingstone. Without self-discipline, the ability to act on every desire can lead to disaster. Many overnight successes in sports and entertainment fall prey to vices like alcohol and drugs, emboldened by their wealth. Their unchecked desires eventually lead them astray.

Though discipline should be a guiding principle for both individuals and organisations, it is often seen as outdated, reserved for the military or police, while creative freedom is valued even in routine tasks. Flexible work hours, holidays, and perks have become more common, often with little regard for productivity.

In today's society, even disciplining children is considered controversial. In the past, parents and teachers played a crucial role in instilling discipline. When success is achieved without discipline, it can lead to boastfulness and serve as a poor example, as seen with some celebrities.

In earlier times, religion often provided structure, setting rules such as abstaining from alcohol or certain foods. Now, with less reliance on religion and a focus on individual freedom, many people lack both faith and self-discipline.

Behind every great success story is a foundation of discipline and hard work. Whether in sports, music, cinema, or investments, reaching the top requires unwavering commitment and sacrifice.

How do we avoid bad habits and build good ones? By shaping our environment to reduce temptations, surrounding ourselves with people we admire, and modelling their positive behaviours.

Discipline is not a burden—embrace it as a lifelong ally!

CHAPTER 56

NEW ERA CASTEISM

In the past, your life path was largely determined by the caste you were born into—Brahmin, Kshatriya, Vaishya, or Shudra. Today, this caste system has transformed into one defined by where you pursued higher education. Whether it's an IIT, NIT, a government engineering college, or a private one in India, or institutions like Oxford, Harvard, Yale, or Stanford in the West, these schools now shape your opportunities. Their powerful alumni networks often give their graduates a significant edge in career advancement.

Graduates from lesser-known colleges frequently struggle to secure the same career opportunities as their counterparts from prestigious institutions. Even when they do, they are often paid much less, despite performing the same roles. Many students take on massive loans to finance their education, only to find themselves burdened by student debt for decades.

For many, after taxes, rent, and repaying student loans, there's little left for basic survival. The cost of higher education has become a financial trap. In India, only the wealthy can truly afford it, making the return on investment questionable at best. In Western countries, many students don't even pursue higher education beyond high school because the costs are simply unaffordable.

Rather than focusing solely on expensive degrees, the real key to success in today's world is skill development. In a skill-driven economy, there are numerous ways to acquire valuable talents—whether it's creative writing, video editing, fitness training, or financial education—that can lead to sustainable income. The focus shouldn't just be on getting a degree. Prioritise acquiring skills that will enable you to thrive in the real world.

CHAPTER 57

GOODWILL OF NEIGHBOURS

I am very cautious when it comes to upgrading my lifestyle. I evaluate the feasibility multiple times, always asking myself: Can I still afford this if I lose my job? Only if the answer is a confident yes do I move forward with the decision.

Last week, after living in the same place for 10 years, we moved to a more spacious location. I assumed it would be a routine move, but the experience held some surprises.

I hired the most expensive movers, assuming that paying more would ensure better service, but I was mistaken. They damaged a lot of our furniture, and their liability wasn't clearly defined.

It turns out, paying a high price doesn't always guarantee better products or services. These workers are often paid very low wages for long hours with minimal benefits. Hearing their stories moved us, so we ordered food for them over the three days they worked for us.

As we were moving out, our neighbours — whom we had only interacted with in passing, mostly in the lobby or elevator — expressed surprise and disappointment. I believe they were from Syria and Yemen. They said, "You were such great neighbours.

We loved your Diwali decorations and the other colourful Indian festivals."

Our Bangladeshi cleaner, employed by the FMS, was even more vocal: "Saab, sab achhe log building chhod ke nahi jaana chahiye" (Good people like you shouldn't leave the building). And the Nepali security guard asked, "Why are you moving? What problem do you have here? We can fix it."

We were taken aback by these reactions, as we thought the world had grown indifferent and no one really cared.

Your true wealth lies in the goodwill of the people around you. Invest in equity, yes — but also invest in people!

CHAPTER 58

FLEXIBILITY – KEEP EVOLVING

"In 1981, a survey of MBA graduates revealed that 80% desired to have families, 73% were willing to serve in the military, and 75% planned to remain in their local towns or villages.

However, by 2021, the priorities of these graduates had shifted dramatically. Only 40% expressed a desire to have families, and the same percentage were willing to die for their country. Additionally, few intended to stay in their home countries, let alone their villages. The most important factor in their decision-making had risen from 29% to 73%: money.

As human beings evolve, so too do their needs, wants, values, and norms (or at least their acceptability).

When I returned from Japan, time discipline was one of my core values. Anyone who arrived late to work received a memo, and any vendor who missed a scheduled meeting lost their opportunity. Over time, however, I realised that such strict adherence to time was not feasible in this part of the world.

Furthermore, companies began offering flexible hours and remote work options, further challenging the traditional value of time discipline. I learned to adapt and be more flexible in my approach to these and other values and norms.

As a leader, it is essential to continuously evolve and avoid clinging to outdated beliefs.

What is one value that you have changed over time?"

CHAPTER 59

ADAPTABILITY – CHANGE WITH TIME

A few months ago, we celebrated our 29th wedding anniversary. Ours was an arranged marriage. Back then, in our community, dating was strictly off-limits, and I was more focused on my studies and career. So, when my parents were searching for a suitable match, there were many filters: she had to be strictly vegetarian (preferably not eating onions or garlic), from the same Vaishnav community, and of a similar economic background, among other criteria.

Now, 29 years later, as we look for suitable matches for our nieces and nephews spread across the globe, all those filters have all but disappeared. The dilution of requirements goes something like this:

- Any Vaishnav girl or boy is fine.
- Any Gujarati girl or boy is fine.
- Any Indian girl or boy is fine.
- Anything, as long as it's not a same-sex marriage, is fine.

But just the other day, a cousin announced he was gay, and we were quick to respond, "Hey, great to know! When's the wedding?

We'll be there to celebrate!" How much has life changed in just 29-30 years? In the past, social and cultural changes happened at a slower pace, giving us time to psychologically adapt. Now, with the advent of technology, these changes occur so rapidly—in every sphere, be it cultural, social, business-related, or otherwise — that I'm not sure we can mentally keep up.

Other day, I overheard one of my European colleague that my husband Son (from his first wife) is getting married to my daughter (from my second marriage)." I thought to myself, "I'm not ready for this yet—are you?" But I've learned that I have to adapt. I need to adjust to all the changes happening in culture, management, leadership, business, and the environment, or else risk becoming irrelevant.

- If you want to get along with your new daughter-in-law, you need to change and adapt.

- If you want to thrive under a new leader at work, you need to change and adapt.

- If you want to stay healthy, you need to adapt to a new sugar-free diet.

Throughout life, we must continually change and adapt. If anyone accepts you without expecting you to change—that's pure love, and it's incredibly rare. Aside from a mother's love, who else will give you that?

So, when I heard that line again — "My husband's son (from his first wife) is marrying my daughter (from my second marriage)" — I asked myself, "Am I ready for this yet?" I'm not there yet — are you?

CHAPTER 60

PURPOSE OF LIFE

―――◆―――

Completed reading "Ikigai" by Nio Maji, a Japanese author. "Ikigai" translates to "reason for being." The book posits that individuals who live purposeful lives tend to enjoy longevity and well-being. It provides examples of numerous ordinary Japanese people leading simple yet meaningful lives. Some find joy in perfecting their craft, such as sushi making or temple service, over many years.

I've often pondered the question of life's purpose, even before reading this book. Despite extensive reflection, I've struggled to find a definitive answer. Initially, survival itself seems to be the primary goal. However, this purpose evolves over time.

In my twenties, I aspired to become an engineer. In my thirties, I sought a stable job with a multinational corporation. In my forties, I aimed to settle abroad and achieve financial security. In my fifties, I dreamed of becoming a millionaire.

Yet, these are merely life goals, not the ultimate purpose. They serve as stepping stones rather than the final destination. The question of life's purpose remains unanswered. Many believe that life is devoid of inherent purpose, and we simply drift along, guided by circumstances. However, such a perspective can lead to aimlessness and depression.

Discovering one's life purpose is a personal journey. While accumulating wealth is a common pursuit, it cannot be the sole purpose. Money is a means to an end, not the end itself. For me, money is a tool to make a positive impact on others' lives, beginning with my loved ones and extending to the broader community.

Recently, while reading a remarkable book, a profound insight emerged regarding life's purpose:

- A healthy and happy body
- A calm and peaceful mind
- Loving friends and family
- Making a positive impact on others' lives
- A painless death

P.S. I added the last point after witnessing my parents' suffering from cancer in their late eighties. The pain they endured was truly unimaginable.

CHAPTER 61

LEGACY

Close your eyes and imagine attending your own funeral, with the unique ability to hear the thoughts of those gathered — your family, friends, and colleagues. What are they thinking about you? This powerful exercise from Stephen Covey's "The 7 Habits of Highly Effective People" shifted my perspective on life and leadership.

Now, take this reflection further. Picture yourself at your retirement farewell, listening to the unspoken thoughts of your team. What are they remembering about you? Are they honouring you as a leader who inspired and empowered them, or are their memories different?

Consider the story of a retired Managing Director from a major Indian bank. Two years into retirement, he revisited a branch he once led, only to find that the staff didn't recognise him. The clerk, peon, and cashier treated him like any other customer until he introduced himself. Their response was polite but telling: "Sir, you're in the priority queue, but your efficiency initiatives cut our workforce. Now, we don't have enough people to maintain those systems. Please be patient."

As a leader, the legacy you leave behind isn't just about the systems you built or the profits you generated — it's about how you shaped the future for those who followed. Did you invest in their growth, ensuring they were equipped for the challenges ahead? Did you leave behind a culture of trust, resilience, and empathy? Because, in the end, your true legacy will be defined not just by what you achieved, but by the lasting impact you had on the people who continue your work, long after you've retired or even passed away.

On a more personal note, consider your own parents or grandparents. Many families have stories of a father or mother who quietly sacrificed to ensure their children had a better future — whether it was working long hours, moving to another city, or making personal compromises. My own father, for example, worked tirelessly to provide for us, teaching us the importance of hard work and honesty, values that continue to guide my decisions today. My mother, on the other hand, taught us empathy and the importance of relationships, instilling in us the need to care for others, even when life gets busy.

A highly successful father – who has no time for his children or highly educated mother who is busy with her kitty parties – what legacy you are living behind for your children? If you are not taking care of your old parents – do you think they are going to take care of you? Look at the Legacy.

In the end, the legacy you leave within your family will be measured not by material success but by the values, lessons, and love that you pass on to the next generation. How you handle everyday moments, how you support each other in times of need, and how you live your values will define your legacy far more than any title or accomplishment.

CHAPTER 62

SHRADDHA – REMEBERING OUR OWN

In many cultures, including Indian traditions, the ritual of recalling seven generations during the last rites carries profound meaning. This act symbolises the recognition of our family's interconnectedness through time and honours the legacies of our ancestors. Unfortunately, we often fail to appreciate the wisdom, resilience, and values passed down through generations.

The irony is clear: while we focus on fleeting social obligations and material celebrations, we often neglect the deeper significance of our familial heritage. Our ancestors, whose sacrifices and efforts laid the foundation for our existence, deserve more than a passing mention. Yet, as generations move forward, memories fade, stories are forgotten, and names disappear into oblivion.

Still, we persist in planning social events, concerned with questions like, "What will people think?" We worry about the quality of food at our weddings or throwing extravagant parties. Why do we care so much about the opinions of others when, in just a few years, even those closest to us might forget these details?

We chase after temporary pleasures and superficial approval, all while remaining disconnected from the rich history of our families.

This could be a reflection of modern life — a preference for the immediate over the enduring, the tangible over the intangible. But in our pursuit of progress and prosperity, we risk losing touch with our roots, disconnecting from the essence of who we are.

Yet, there is hope. It's never too late to reconnect with our familial heritage, to dive into the stories of those who came before us, and to honour their memories by preserving their legacies.

By actively remembering, celebrating, and passing on our family history, we not only pay tribute to our ancestors but also enrich our own lives with a deeper sense of belonging and identity.

So, let us pause amidst the noise of modern life and take a moment to remember and cherish the timeless wisdom of our ancestors. By doing so, we not only honour the past but also pave the way for a more meaningful and grounded future.

CHAPTER 63

NOTHING – ZERO EGO

Person 1: "Can I supply some plastics and steel drums, chemicals to your company?" I replied, "We don't require those materials. We specialise in EPC projects."

Person 2: "Can I supply some EOT cranes for your company? We manufacture them in India." I responded, "That sounds promising, but we need to ensure compliance with AVL regulations. You'll need to complete all necessary formalities before we can consider your proposal."

Person 3: "You're hiring a lot these days. Can you give my son a job?" I requested, "Please have him submit an application. Our HR department will contact him if he's a suitable candidate."

Regrettably, I couldn't assist any of these individuals, despite our personal connections. When they gathered together, they concluded that I held no significant influence within the company. And I must humbly agree. I am indeed insignificant. I was of little consequence in school, college, society, or business. I am simply an ordinary engineer, content with my current circumstances. I compete against myself daily, not against others. I can offer assistance, but I cannot guarantee favourable outcomes.

Every large company has certain procedures and requirements. Any manager has to follow those guidelines. Even if you are Purchasing Director, you simply can not buy any material from any supplier at any cost. You can not offer everyone a job. You have lots of limitations in large organisation.

Are you a person of consequence, or are you like me — A Nothing?

CHAPTER 64

WINNING WAR LOSING BATTLES

As a procurement professional, negotiations are a core part of life. But in reality, everyone negotiates in one way or another throughout their lives. Life itself is a continuous series of struggles and negotiations. You negotiate with your kids — "Finish your homework, and I'll give you chocolate." It's simple but still a negotiation. Life is full of such interactions with the people around you.

But is it possible to win every negotiation? Can every negotiation result in a win-win outcome? The truth is, you can't win them all. Sometimes, you have to accept losses. I often deliberately give up in negotiations because it's important to focus on the bigger picture.

For example, once my family and I were headed to one of the most expensive resorts in India for a holiday. I had agreed on a fixed rate with the driver, but upon arrival, he demanded much more than what we had settled on. Did I argue or negotiate with him? No. I decided to let it go, keeping in mind that we were on vacation, and I didn't want to ruin the mood right from the start.

You don't need to pick every small fight. Be willing to lose a battle in order to win the war. In our professional lives, too, we can't push everything onto the supplier. Sometimes, we need to let go of small things and focus on the bigger picture. When you give up on minor points, the supplier feels more satisfied. It's important to consciously leave room for something you are willing to concede.

Consider a businessman who, well-versed in the concept of opportunity cost, chooses to work late every night instead of spending time with his family. Over time, he alienates them and eventually becomes distanced from his loved ones.

While working late might have helped him win the "battle" of business, what about the "war" of life? Sadly, many people realise too late that the price they paid for their success was far too high.

CHAPTER 65

EXPECTATIONS SETTING

Yesterday, while attempting to adjust my phone's settings to limit screen time, I realised a thought-provoking parallel: Could we also modify the settings of our lives? Is it possible to reduce greed to a minimum, moderate expectations, and maximise joy from small things?

Expectations are a double-edged sword, influencing both our self-perception and the expectations others hold for us. While we often find satisfaction in our achievements despite challenges, friends, family, and society often demand more. Questions like "Why aren't you a vice president yet?" or "Why are you still driving a Pajero?" are commonplace in my experience.

I firmly believe in setting low expectations and exceeding them. As an investor, my market expectations are modest, aiming for a return slightly above fixed deposit rates without risking capital. However, I've been pleasantly surprised to achieve over 12% returns for the past 16 years.

Managing expectations to a minimum and exceeding them leads to pleasant surprises. In the stock market, there are companies that underpromise and overdeliver (like UBS), those that deliver on their promises (like TITAN), and those that fall short (like ITC).

Similarly, in relationships, promising the moon and stars initially can lead to disappointment when reality falls short. The adage "under promise and overdeliver" holds true in various aspects of life.

This Diwali, let's set our expectations right and embrace the joy of exceeding them.

CHAPTER 66

PEACE OR JUSTICE

I met Aaditi, a brilliant and level-headed college classmate. Despite her professional success working with renowned brands and earning a substantial income, her personal life has been fraught with challenges. She has separated from her husband and estranged herself from her family, now living alone with her son after numerous job changes.

Aaditi's perfectionism can be both a strength and a weakness. While she strives for excellence in everything she does, her uncompromising nature can lead to conflicts and difficulties. I tried to persuade her that life is inherently imperfect and that flexibility is essential. While compromising on one's moral or ethical values is unacceptable, a certain degree of compromise is often necessary to navigate life's complexities.

Throughout history, treaties and agreements have typically been reached through compromise. The pursuit of absolute justice can often lead to endless conflict and suffering. Consider the numerous ongoing wars, fuelled by a refusal to compromise. Even within families, disagreements over seemingly insignificant matters can escalate into long-standing feuds.

For me, mental peace takes precedence over absolute justice at this stage of my life. I believe that a harmonious existence is more valuable than the pursuit of an unattainable ideal.

Do you prioritise mental peace or absolute justice?

CHAPTER 67

COACHING ADVANTAGE

"Another coach for you?" I couldn't help but laugh as I agreed, after hiring a diet and exercise coach just yesterday. I didn't have this many tutors back in school! But yes, I've relied on individual coaches throughout much of my life. I have a financial coach, a life coach, and now, a diet coach.

To me, a coach is like a catalyst in a chemical reaction. While two elements might interact on their own, the presence of a catalyst accelerates the process significantly. Real-world examples abound: think of a world-class athlete who, despite their natural talent, still depends on a coach to refine their skills and push their performance to new heights.

In today's world, flooded with information on health, finance, and investments, making the right decisions can feel like navigating a maze. Much like a skilled navigator is crucial for a ship in uncharted waters, a coach serves as a compass, guiding you through complexities with their expertise and experience.

Looking back at historical figures, take Steve Jobs, for instance. Despite being an iconic innovator, he sought mentorship from individuals like Robert Friedland, showing how even the most brilliant minds benefit from guidance.

Similarly, companies like Apple and Google didn't achieve their success solely on individual brilliance. Their visionary leaders surrounded themselves with coaches and advisors to help navigate challenges and seize opportunities.

As someone who tends to be frugal, my significant investment in coaching isn't just an expense — it's a strategic decision to navigate life's complexities. I see it as hiring a team of experts to ensure continuous growth and learning.

Just as **Arjun** had **Shri Krishn** by his side during the **Mahabharata,** I recognise the value of having professional guides to help me on my own journey!

CHAPTER 68

HARD WORK – DO IT!!

I've always been a dedicated worker. To achieve 90% marks in my Class X, XII, and Engineering exams, I consistently studied for twelve hours a day. The daily commute from Karjat to Dadar on the 4:30 AM local train was a gruelling part of my routine.

Early in my career, I worked on demanding petrochemical and power projects. These greenfield developments often required long hours and tight deadlines. I frequently put in twelve-hour days, six days a week, and commuted five years between Karjat and Cuffe Parade, spending six hours daily in transit.

My overseas assignments in Japan and the UAE presented even more challenging work cultures. In Japan, the standard workday was from 8:30 AM to 7:30 PM, five days a week. The UAE offered demanding projects and a competitive work environment. To succeed in these roles, hard work was essential.

While natural talent can be beneficial, I believe that hard work and honesty are fundamental for personal and professional growth. The more you work, the more you learn. My motivation to work hard wasn't solely driven by my manager's expectations but by my commitment to fulfilling my responsibilities.

The extent of your dedication depends on factors like age, needs, position, and personal passion. No one should dictate your work ethic. Your future is in your hands. By working hard and persistently, you can achieve success without taking shortcuts.

CHAPTER 69

EXECUTION OR STRATEGY

When EPC (Engineering, Procurement, and Construction) companies bid for large tenders, they often form joint ventures with other EPC firms to share risks and leverage each other's expertise. Interestingly, these same companies might collaborate on one project while competing fiercely against each other for another. I used to wonder: how does this work? Aren't they competitors? Won't they learn each other's tactics and use them in future bids?

It's similar to sports, where coaches, players, and managers switch teams frequently. For example, Hardik Pandya captained Gujarat Titans (GT) in one season and then transferred to Mumbai Indians (MI) in the next. Wouldn't he carry GT's strategies with him to MI? Or look at Gautam Gambhir, who mentored Lucknow Super Giants (LSG), but now returns to Kolkata Knight Riders (KKR). Don't these frequent changes expose so-called "secret strategies"?

The answer is simpler than it seems: strategies aren't the secret to success—execution is. In both sports and business, there are no exclusive formulas or revolutionary tactics that guarantee a win. What sets winners apart is their ability to flawlessly execute their strategies, day in and day out.

Take Walmart, for example. Its core strategy is simple: provide the lowest prices through operational efficiency and massive scale. Thousands of businesses know this strategy, but few can replicate it because they can't match Walmart's relentless execution of lean operations, vendor negotiations, and supply chain optimisation.

In another case, Apple's success doesn't come from a secret marketing strategy—it comes from its consistent ability to deliver high-quality products with a seamless customer experience. Many tech companies know the elements of Apple's approach, but few can execute at the same level.

Amazon is yet another example where execution trumps strategy. Their customer-first approach and obsession with fast, reliable delivery are well-known strategies. Competitors like eBay or Walmart have attempted to adopt similar models, but what sets Amazon apart is its relentless investment in infrastructure, logistics, and technological innovation, ensuring flawless execution of that strategy.

As a procurement leader, I'm often asked, "What's your strategy?" For me, it has remained the same for the last 30 years: source materials at the lowest cost from technically qualified vendors. The true challenge isn't the strategy itself but the execution—securing the most competitive offers, leveraging specifications and the AVL (Approved Vendor List), building strong vendor relationships, and managing the flow of information. Success lies in how well you execute these aspects daily.

In corporate boardrooms, strategy is often overhyped. While it's important, it's not enough. Google didn't become the leader in search just because of a brilliant strategy—it became the leader because of its ability to constantly improve and deliver relevant results through precise execution. Similarly, Tesla didn't revolutionise the electric vehicle market with a strategy alone; it executed on innovations in battery technology, design, and scalability.

To sum it up, while strategy is critical, it's merely the starting point. The real game is won in execution. Without it, even the best-laid plans remain just that—plans. Success in both business and sports isn't about having the most secretive strategy; it's about who can execute that strategy consistently and with excellence.

CHAPTER 70

BIG BAKWAAS

The other day, I was asked to attend an Ethics & Compliance webinar to obtain a certificate. I wondered, why do I need this? After all, my Indian middle-class upbringing has already instilled strong values in me — don't smoke, don't drink alcohol, don't eat meat, and always be a law-abiding, tax-paying citizen. What more could I need?

But wait. When it comes to business, ethics and compliance are an entirely different ball game. Take the food industry, for instance. Despite knowing that sugar is harmful to health, they still manage to sell billions of dollars worth of cold drinks and ice cream.

The dairy and meat industries continue to profit massively each year, even though they are fully aware that killing animals for profit is unethical. The pharmaceutical industry, too, often prescribes unnecessary medications, knowing it's of little benefit to the patient and may even lead to harmful dependencies. Yet, they do it anyway.

Personally, I was sold as many as five different insurance policies by a reputed bank in India, even though they knew those policies didn't suit my needs. For industries, ethics often boil down to staying within the boundaries of laws — laws that, more often than not, are crafted by policymakers they sponsor, while raking in billions.

And here we are, needing to get certified by them on ethics. The irony is palpable. Stick to your own set of ethics and values.

The rest is just **badi badi baatien and Bakwaas** (big talk and nonsense).

CHAPTER 71

FINE PRINTS

How many of us actually read the terms and conditions written in fine print before downloading software or making purchases from online platforms? I believe very few do. When I worked as a Junior Executive in smaller companies, I made it a point to carefully read all the T&Cs. However, once I joined a large corporation, I found myself imposing our T&Cs on others and gradually lost the habit of reading the fine print on offers.

Recently, while traveling to Ahmedabad, I had a ticket that allowed 30 kg of baggage. Having traveled with this airline regularly, I didn't expect any surprises. My baggage was only 20 kg, so I thought everything was in order. But when I reached the check-in counter, they asked me to pay an extra AED 80. Even though my total baggage weight was well below the limit, I had two bags instead of one.

My arguments didn't sway them, and in the end, I had to pay the extra AED 80. Logic, physics, engineering—none of it mattered against the airline's rigid rules. I wasn't alone; many others faced the same predicament. It was especially disheartening to see blue-collar workers, who can barely read, endure such unnecessary hardships.

Large corporations have immense power, and they often crush us under the weight of their terms and conditions. What choice do we have if we don't agree with the T&Cs of Google, Facebook, or Instagram? None. We're powerless to challenge them. Another area where fine print is often abused is in insurance policies. I've fallen victim to this many times. Have you ever been caught by the small print and would like to share your experience? How long will these mighty corporations continue to extort money from the common man?

CHAPTER 72

STEPS TOWARDS LEADERSHIP

A) Take Initiative – Be Enterprising:

Bring fresh ideas to the table. Take initiative by starting new projects, proposing innovative solutions, and creating new opportunities for the business. Be adaptable to meet any project requirements and drive success.

B) Be Ready to Learn:

Regardless of which college you attended or your CGPA, be prepared to learn. The technology sector is evolving at a rapid pace. Show your manager that you are coachable, attentive, and always eager to acquire new skills.

C) Anticipate Needs:

Stay one step ahead of your team by asking yourself, "If I were my boss, what would I want done next?" This demonstrates a proactive, go-getter attitude.

D) Effective Communication:

Proactively communicate with your team. Let them know when a task is completed and what needs to be done next. Avoid surprises. Never sweep problems under the rug.

E) Actions Speak Volumes:

Actions hold far more weight than words. Use this principle at work. Rather than boasting about what you can do, focus on delivering results. Show management what you are capable of through your actions.

F) Gain Trust – Be Honest with All Stakeholders:

Trust is critical, especially in supply chain management. You need to earn the trust of both management and suppliers through honesty and transparency.

G) Create Solutions:

No one cares about your degree, grade, or title. What matters to your manager is your ability to solve the problem at hand.

H) Empathy – Be Compassionate:

Show empathy to everyone—whether it's your team members, internal customers, or external clients. Help others to the extent possible, and it will return to you manyfold.

CHAPTER 73

COMPANY EXPENSES

During my time at IHI in Japan, extensive travel was a regular part of my role. My trips primarily focused on Asian countries, including China, India, Malaysia, and Indonesia.

In the past, I enjoyed the luxury of business class flights and five-star hotels. However, for domestic or regional travel, I preferred to opt for more economical options. In India, the exorbitant cost of five-star hotels (around USD 400 per night in New Delhi) made them impractical. Instead, I often stayed in company guesthouses and used taxis for local transportation.

This cost-saving approach, however, met with resistance from my colleagues. They believed that company funds were meant to be used without hesitation and questioned my motives for conserving resources.

A similar incident occurred during a six-month project in the United States. While my colleagues opted for individual hotel rooms at a cost of USD 110 per day, I shared a hotel apartment with another colleague for only USD 100 per day. This decision again sparked disapproval from my peers, who felt I was depriving them of their right to spend company money.

I approach every job with a business-oriented mindset. If I were responsible for the company's profits and losses, I would carefully consider every expenditure. Would I splurge or save money? The answer is clear: I would prioritise savings without compromising on comfort or safety.

Everyone has their own lifestyle preferences. While it's essential to adhere to company guidelines regarding maximum spending, there's no shame in saving money when possible. A company is made up of individuals like us. Many of my former bosses and their families who once held positions of power and enjoyed unlimited company perks are now suffering due to spoiled habits after retirement.

CHAPTER 74

POOR ENGINEERS

———◆———

Engineers design products and software that benefit humanity. They also design, build, and oversee complex projects that serve the same purpose. As the company grows, engineers hire professionals from various fields, such as finance, law, quality assurance, safety, information technology, and human resources, to support its operations.

Initially, these support functions work seamlessly to contribute to the company's success. However, as the company expands and goes public, finance professionals often become Chief Financial Officers (CFOs), legal experts become Chief Legal Officers (CLOs), human resources specialists become Chief People Officers (CPOs), and information technology professionals become Chief Information Officers (CIOs).

With these new titles and increased influence, these support functions may sometimes prioritise their own areas of expertise over the overall business goals. As a result, engineers, who are often the foundation of the company, may find themselves marginalised and overlooked.

CHAPTER 75

BIRDS & HUMANS

Every morning when I go for a walk along the Sharjah Corniche, I see a variety of birds. These birds naturally form their own groups. Grey pigeons flock together, black crows form their own group, and white pigeons, which are usually migratory, have their own club.

The Maina and Koyal have their own distinct dance. Each group of birds segregates itself based on its unique characteristics.

The other day, I attended a professional company's party. During the networking session, I noticed a similar pattern — Indians gathered in their own group, discussing the stock market; Middle Easterners formed their own circle, talking about the Israel-Gaza conflict; and Europeans were busy chatting about the best wines in the world.

Even when we Indians meet, we tend to further segregate by state — Gujarati, Marathi, Punjabi, and so on. And within the Gujarati group, we split again into Baroda, Surat, and Dahod groups.

This habit of forming groups based on shared characteristics is so natural, almost instinctual. But in the corporate world, especially when working in diverse environments, we are expected to demonstrate inclusion and embrace diversity.

We can't behave like birds and animals. Some British expert then has to come in and train people on diversity and inclusion.

Who's going to tell those migratory white pigeons that there are some smart black pigeons who can help them navigate the treacherous Siberian journey without losing a life?

Ever wonder why many company boards lack representation from people of colour? I believe it's instinct — just like the birds on my morning walk.

CHAPTER 76

LESSONS FROM A LIZARD

It's rare to find a lizard in a residential flat in the Middle East, especially when living in well-maintained, high-rise buildings. In mid-January 2022, after returning from a shopping trip at night, my wife saw something darting quickly into the shadows. I brushed it off, telling her it was just her phobia. But the next morning, as she opened the curtains, a lizard suddenly dropped onto her head, terrifying her.

She has a fear of all small, fast-moving creatures like lizards and cockroaches. For the next two hours, she was frozen in place.

My daughter and I, on the other hand, didn't mind sharing the space with the lizard. After all, it has just as much right to be on this Earth (though maybe not in our flat). While we remained calm and unbothered, my wife was extremely distressed. She spotted it two or three more times over the following week, but neither my daughter nor I ever saw it ourselves.

Later, when my wife and daughter went to India for six weeks, I didn't see the lizard even once. I confidently sent a message: **"Some problems, if ignored, resolve themselves."**

I assumed the lizard had wandered away through the AC ducts or something. But as soon as my wife returned from India, she found two of them in the bathroom. This time, it was her turn to lecture me: **"Some problems, if ignored, multiply."**

The next day, I Googled "lizard control" and to my surprise, such services existed! The pest control team came, caught both lizards, and charged AED 500. But my wife was relieved—and when my wife is relieved, the whole household is at peace.

Lessons:

1. You get exactly what you search for.

2. For every problem, there are experts. You just have to look for them.

CHAPTER 77

GORI MADAM

From mid-2007 to mid-2009, I was on an assignment in Tampa, Florida, staying at a Marriott hotel on a long-term lease, right next to our office.

Every day, I would go to the Marriott gym and spend about 45 minutes on the treadmill. There, I often saw a woman, probably in her late 60s, doing heavy lifting and other intense exercises. At the time, I was in my early 40s, and I found it hard to believe that someone her age could manage such strenuous workouts.

After seeing her for a while, I finally asked her one day, "Why are you doing such heavy exercises?" She bluntly replied, "I can't afford to lose muscle strength at my age, you know."

During that same period, we used to visit a Gujarati restaurant run by the Patel family, where we'd enjoy a full Thali for just USD 7. There was another regular customer — an American woman around the same age as the lady in the gym — but she suddenly stopped coming. One day, I saw her again and casually asked, "Why did you stop coming to the Indian restaurant?" She answered, "Lack of protein."

At the time, I thought to myself, "These women are crazy. They don't know anything about health."

Fast forward to yesterday: I had my first session with a diet and exercise coach. His first advice to me was, "Mr. Shah, as you're aging, we need to focus on resistance training and a protein-rich diet."

Life had come full circle. If I had listened to that lady back then, I'd likely be in much better shape today.

Not all our traditions and assumptions hold true forever. They need to evolve with time. Still, it's not too late — I'm listening to my trainer now, rather than relying on free advice.

CHAPTER 78

UNPLANNED CHILD

In today's nuclear families, where there's little or no parental support and both partners are often working, raising children can be challenging. Before deciding to take on this responsibility, ensure you're ready to put in the extra effort required.

A) Remember, your children didn't ask to be born — you brought them into this world. When it comes to parenting, there's no room for half-measures. Commit fully.

B) What children crave most is your time and love. These cannot be outsourced. Both parents, or at least one, must consistently spend quality time with them. Even if you're as busy as a CEO, you can still make time for your kids.

C) Never underestimate how perceptive children are. They absorb their surroundings and their parents 'habits unconsciously but deeply. Therefore, it's essential to set the right example in values, ethics, and integrity. Walk the talk!

D) Regardless of how much you may provide, teach them to appreciate the value of money, human dignity, and labor. If they don't understand the effort required to put food on the table, they will struggle to value anything else in life.

E) Above all, instil respect for elders and emphasise how they enrich our lives. As your children grow older, discuss with them the importance of consent and respecting others 'boundaries.

F) Encourage them to be open-minded and value diverse perspectives. Foster healthy debate and discussion, guiding them gently but allowing them to make their own decisions. Let them feel confident that, no matter the situation, their parents will always be there without judgment.

G) Handle any differences between you and your spouse privately — never in front of the children. They should always see their parents as a united, indivisible team. Avoid trying to score points or outshine your partner in front of your kids.

H) Lastly, respect your children's choices, whether in their career, life partner, or any other personal decisions. Remember, they are your children, not your clones.

Give them love, respect, and confidence — it's the greatest gift you can offer!

CHAPTER 79

WORRIED PARENTS

"Why are you so worried about me? I'm already 25!" my daughter shouted when I called to check if everything was okay. I often keep track of them by checking their WhatsApp status, last seen, double ticks, and so on. If for any reason my message doesn't go through (no double ticks), I'll call them. If they don't answer, I'll contact their closest friend.

As a father, your concern for your kids' safety never goes away. I didn't argue; I simply said, "When you become a parent, you'll understand." Before my uncle got married, he lived just two lanes away from us with my grandfather. Whenever my uncle was late returning from work, my 78-year-old grandfather, despite his poor night vision, would go out into the dark streets, worrying about him.

We would try to reassure him, saying, "He must be delayed because of work. He'll be back soon." But my grandfather wouldn't relax — he would sit at our house until my uncle returned.

In those days, we didn't have phones. So, when my grandfather came over looking for my uncle, my mom, being the youngest in the family, would send me out to all my uncle's usual hangouts. I'd either bring him back or return with some news, and only then would my grandfather be at ease.

Have I inherited this parental worry? Or is it just a normal part of being a parent? My partner, on the other hand, stays completely calm and unbothered.

Does this happen to you?

CHAPTER 80

STAYCATION

Although I consciously avoided the rush of the Eid holidays, I opted for a staycation at a resort in RAK last week. However, I belong to a rare breed of individuals who don't particularly enjoy vacations.

The reasons for my dissatisfaction are quite simple:

4. I approach vacations with a corporate mindset, meticulously scheduling every activity. But holidays don't work with rigid timetables; they thrive on spontaneity and relaxation.

5. As an Indian, there's an ingrained urge to cram as many experiences and sights as possible into a holiday. Instead of prioritising rest, the focus shifts to maximising the itinerary. I can't just lie on the beach and sunbathe. Sunbathing? What a funny concept!

6. Since food is included in the room charges, the sheer wastage of food during breakfast was disheartening. Despite being surrounded by well-educated, affluent individuals, the amount of uneaten food left behind was staggering.

7. There's the constant pressure to capture every moment in photographs, as if we're not on a vacation but filming for someone else's benefit. Is it really our holiday, or are we just curating a show for social media?

8. The endless struggle to find satisfactory Indian vegetarian cuisine at resorts only adds to the frustration. My palate lacks diversity, and since I don't drink alcohol, no one seems eager to accompany me.

Still, vacations do break the monotony and sometimes bring peace within the family. At the very least, you get to brag, "Oh! I had a vacation."

My idea of a perfect vacation? Solitude in the Himalayas.

CHAPTER 81

EGO MANAGEMENT

I live in a residential society in India consisting of 18 flats owned by 12 different individuals. The residents fall into three categories: the rich (worth around 1 crore), the super-rich (worth around 5 crores), and the ultra-rich (worth around 10 crores). Given their financial success, it's evident that these individuals are accomplished in their respective professions. But with success often comes ego. It's easy to cross the line from self-respect **(Swabhiman)** to arrogance **(Abhimaan)** without even realising it.

Although there aren't any major conflicts among the members, everyone tends to operate independently. For instance, when it comes to common tasks like appointing 24-hour security, installing solar panels, or upgrading the elevator, no one shows up for discussions. While individual interactions remain cordial, collective decision-making is nearly impossible. There's a lot of talk about environmental conservation and water saving in the society's WhatsApp group, but when it comes to taking real action, nothing happens.

My experience in Japan, where I worked for IHI for three years, was the complete opposite. I found that while individual Japanese people may have average intelligence, when it comes to collective efforts; whether in social, national, or organisational contexts.

They are incredibly united and get things done efficiently. This approach is sorely lacking in Indian society.

In the corporate world, when you have a small team of highly intelligent individuals working together, success isn't just about their knowledge and skills; it's about their attitude, culture, and ego management. When you build teams of highly successful individuals who often work in silos with inflated egos, they struggle to collectively solve complex organisational problems, often leading the organisation to a spectacular failure.

A case in point: three Nobel laureate economists once started a wealth fund that failed miserably — not due to a lack of knowledge or intelligence, but because they couldn't manage their egos. In today's world, solving complex problems requires not only skills, knowledge, and expertise but also a high level of ego management.

Do you have it?

CHAPTER 82

LIFE – FROM DEATH POINT OF VIEW

If I had known my wife would take more than five minutes shopping, I would have gotten a parking ticket. She took 15 minutes, and sure enough, I ended up with a fine. If I had known the tender deadline would be extended, I would have approached the task more systematically and offered sharper prices. But now, an extra week or two is of no use.

"If only I had known"—a common refrain in life. We navigate through endless uncertainties. One thing, however, is certain: if you are born, you will die. Death is inevitable. As a child, I used to solve puzzles in reverse. Finding the treasure was easier if you traced the path backward rather than starting from the beginning and facing numerous obstacles.

In the corporate world, we often work the same way—starting with the end in mind. If the client's projects' completion date is in 36 months, we calculate when we need to place orders for long-lead items.

So, why not approach life's puzzle the same way? I know that one day I will die, and with that in mind, I estimate I have about 10 working years left, followed by 10 years of retirement. Shouldn't I plan my life in reverse?

Plan life from the perspective of death —

A) What do I still need to accomplish?
B) What legacy do I want to leave behind?
C) What will people say about me when I'm no longer here?

CHAPTER 83

WHAT MAKES YOU HAPPY?

Most of the time, I don't know what truly makes me happy. All my life, I've been chasing other people's dreams — my mom wants this, my wife wants that and I never really stop to think about what I want. Recently, I conducted a little experiment, first on myself, then on my family. I asked everyone to list the 10 happiest moments of their lives. Honestly, I struggled to remember the last time I felt genuinely happy.

Acquiring things like a new iPhone or a car has simply become part of a checklist—planned achievements. They don't bring much joy. None of my promotions filled me with happiness either; they were long overdue anyway.

If I had to categorise happiness, I'd broadly divide it into a few areas:

1) Personal Achievements with an Element of Surprise: For instance, receiving an unexpected call from Japan that led to a spontaneous trip, or my daughter calling from the USA to announce she'd been selected by Google — those moments were pure joy.

2) Social Activities with Friends and Family: Events like Garba nights, kite flying festivals, and weddings bring immense happiness through their lively, spontaneous energy. One of my happiest memories is spending a night catching up with my childhood friend.

3) National Pride: Watching India win the World Cup or witnessing a monumental achievement like landing on the moon fills me with collective joy and a sense of unity.

The moment you hand over control of your happiness to someone else, you set yourself up for disappointment. Expecting others to love you, appreciate you, or care for you is a surefire way to feel unhappy. After asking my family to list their happiest moments, I realised how challenging it can be to find genuine happiness these days.

For me, Social gatherings, such as Garba nights, kite festivals, and weddings in the family, bring joy through their spirited and spontaneous atmosphere. Another cherished memory is a night spent with my childhood friends and having honest conversation about everything on the earth. National pride also plays a part in my happiness — moments like India winning the World Cup or reaching significant milestones like landing on the moon fill me with collective joy and unity.

Throughout history, philosophers and thinkers have explored the nature of happiness. Aristotle believed that true happiness lies in fulfilling one's potential and living in accordance with virtue — what he called eudaemonia, or flourishing. Viktor Frankl, in Man's Search for Meaning, argued that happiness comes from finding purpose in life, even in the face of suffering.

What makes you Happy? At this age, if I have clear bowel movement, no gas in the stomach, feeling hungry makes me Happy.

CHAPTER 84

PURPOSE OF OFFICE

It's not my salary that I worry about—what troubles me is the fear of losing my job. My work gives me purpose. It's what gets me out of bed each morning, gets me moving, meeting people, and staying busy contributing to the organisation. Imagine if I earned the same salary but had almost nothing to do—would I still be happy? Absolutely not.

Consider an Indian diplomat working in the USA versus one stationed in Afghanistan. Though they may earn the same salary, who is more likely to enjoy their work? The same applies to an IPS officer managing a large city compared to one assigned to a training school. Humans have a natural desire to stay busy, to be productive, to use our creativity and intellect. I recall a recent vacation, where after 10 or 12 days of beautiful scenery, I was itching to get back to work. Had the vacation lasted another week or two, I might have revolted!

Work itself isn't the issue. The problem arises when work feels meaningless, when office politics turn toxic, or when backstabbing and one-upmanship dominate the environment. What people truly need isn't early retirement—it's better work, better colleagues, or both. Sitting idle is a death sentence for the mind.

CHAPTER 85

FRIENDS & COLLEAGUES

When you have no money, you have no friends. It's a harsh reality that applies equally to individuals and organisations. In large organisations, you interact with many colleagues, building connections based on shared values, culture, language, or region. Some of these connections even blossom into friendships.

But the bitter truth is that most of these so-called friends aren't truly your friends. They're simply there for the ride when it's fun, convenient, or beneficial to them.

There are other bittersweet examples I won't go into detail about — like when you think you're close to someone, yet they completely ignore you when it comes to major celebrations, like a housewarming or their son's wedding. The sting of hypocrisy runs deep in many of these so-called friendships.

I'm in the painful process of cutting ties with such people. Losing colleagues like this is part of growing up. I'd rather have a few genuine friends than be surrounded by those who only stick around when it suits them.

Not everyone is bad. But the moment you change jobs or locations, many of those connections weaken and you're reduced to just another contact in a WhatsApp group. Finding your real friends — the ones who stand by you when you have nothing, no money, no job, no authority — isn't easy. They are your true treasures.

Find them, cherish them, for they will be the ones holding your hand during your darkest hours.

CHAPTER 86

ARGUMENTATIVE INDIA

During my trip to India, I reconnected with many familiar faces—old friends, relatives, schoolmates, and former colleagues. As we gathered, naturally, we found ourselves engrossed in discussions covering a wide range of topics, from the Ukraine-Russia conflict and the Punjab and Uttar Pradesh elections to the Modi-Kejriwal rivalry and the much-talked-about film, **"The Kashmir Files."**

These are the kind of hot-button issues that dominate conversations everywhere these days. And while they are undoubtedly important and fascinating in their own right, I couldn't help but wonder if we were truly making the best use of our time together.

In the moment, these debates felt stimulating, but looking back, I realise that much of it was just noise. We ended up investing hours into discussions that, while interesting, ultimately led nowhere. These are matters that are largely beyond our control, and engaging in them often only adds fuel to existing divisions.

Instead of focusing on controversial, divisive topics that can easily escalate into heated arguments, wouldn't it have been more enriching if we had spent our time exchanging ideas that directly impact our personal growth?

Imagine the difference if, instead of arguing over political rivalries or international conflicts, we had shared our most recent learning experiences — whether it's a new skill we've picked up, an inspiring book we've read, or even our personal strategies for navigating career goals or planning for retirement.

These are conversations that have the power to motivate, uplift, and truly benefit us as individuals. They move us toward our goals rather than pulling us into debates that waste valuable time and energy.

I've come to believe that we, as a generation, spend far too much time fixated on matters that don't directly affect our personal or professional lives. These topics, while tempting to discuss, often overshadow the more pressing issues that deserve our attention — our own ambitions, our dreams, and the goals we've set for ourselves.

What if, instead of arguing about politics or films, we redirected that energy toward discussing how to improve ourselves or what steps we're taking to achieve our aspirations? We could even go a step further by sharing our goals with one another, creating a sense of public accountability that drives us to stay committed and focused.

Not all conversations are lost causes, though. One thing I've always appreciated about gatherings with fellow Gujaratis is that, more often than not, our discussions naturally gravitate toward emerging industries, new technologies, and business opportunities. We talk about investments, about the future.

But even then, there's a tendency to focus primarily on wealth creation, as though making money is the ultimate goal. Many people believe that if you have enough money, you can simply hire the right people to fill in the knowledge gaps, to do the thinking for you.

But I would argue that knowledge sharing is just as important — if not more so—than the pursuit of wealth. The real value lies not in how much money we accumulate, but in how much wisdom we gain along the way and how that knowledge can be used to create lasting impact.

Conversations that revolve around learning and exchanging ideas can be just as fruitful, if not more so, than those that centre purely on financial gain.

In the end, there's no denying that Gujaratis have a unique knack for success, and yes, Gujjus do rock! But perhaps it's time we not only rock the business world but also build a culture of sharing knowledge and learning, inspiring one another to grow in ways that go beyond monetary wealth.

By shifting our focus from fleeting arguments to meaningful, productive conversations, we can collectively drive ourselves toward a more fulfilling and purpose-driven life.

CHAPTER 87

WEDDING PLANNER

As a Purchaser, I initially believed that buying from an Agent or agency-recommended vendor might lead to inflated prices due to commissions. However, my recent experience with a wedding planner completely changed my perspective.

Despite reservations, I decided to explore the vendors recommended by my planner. Surprisingly, I found them to offer superior deals, the latest brands, and substantial discounts, even at branded stores. The logic is simple: These vendors likely provide consistent business to the planner.

For NRIs with limited time, a reliable wedding planner is invaluable. By following their recommendations, you can significantly save time and avoid the overwhelming task of exploring countless options. While the joy of browsing can be appealing, it's often unnecessary when dealing with the multitude of choices for clothes, dresses, jewellery, return gifts, makeup artists, mehendi artists, and performers.

Indian weddings are notoriously demanding, not just financially but also emotionally. Stress levels tend to escalate as the event approaches, and families often struggle to reach a consensus amidst numerous options. The constant worry of societal judgment ("Log Kya Kahenge") can add to the pressure.

To save time and reduce stress, consider hiring an honest wedding planner and following their recommendations. Their management fees are well worth the investment compared to the time and energy spent exploring options.

Our family was so impressed with our planner's dedication and efforts that we willingly paid a significantly higher fee than initially agreed. Their invaluable assistance in planning our memorable event was truly priceless.

CHAPTER 88

MARRIAGE MARKET

It is boom season for Indian Wedding Industry which is worth USD 50 billion annually.

Everyone is trying to over smart everyone else with some additional event, dance, food, location. Earlier, people who were getting married at home are moving to Hotel Banquet, Hotel Banquet category is moving to resorts and resort people are moving overseas. This is so widespread that even PM has to question – is it necessary to go abroad and spend money?

There is nothing wrong with the Grand Celebration. People who have money can certainly celebrate and announce to the world that they have arrived. It is mostly show of your money power to impress social circle.

But if the middle-class Indian families are just doing it by taking loan or using retirement funds – it is not a sound financial decision. As a parent, you have the responsibility to raise and educate – not to spend Crores – at the cost of your retirement fund.

I was also ready to spend big bang for my daughter marriage, but both she and her finance decided to get married in the court (both Googlers).

There simple response was it is your money – you spend on you and I have no mental space. This mental space is new word for me – in Gujarati it is called magajmari.

If you are getting married – ask yourself a question – whose money it is? And whose mental space?

CHAPTER 89

SUSTAINABILITY

Growing up in India, I had an older brother who would wear his school uniform for 2-3 years, and then it would be passed down to me. I'd wear it for another 2-3 years, after which the shirt would be repurposed into a quilt or used for kitchen cleaning, and the pants would become rags for cleaning the bicycle.

Once they were thoroughly soaked in grease and oil, they were given their final role: fuelling the **chulha** (stove).

Our approach to sustainability wasn't a conscious, trendy choice — it was born out of necessity in the face of poverty. Fast forward to today's Indian weddings, and they've become a Bollywood fashion spectacle on steroids.

Every ceremony — **Mehendi, Haldi, Sangeet, Baraat,** and Reception demands its own wardrobe. It's like playing fashion Tetris, but with more pressure, societal expectations, and the fear of being photographed in the same outfit twice on Instagram.

So, what happens to these extravagantly expensive outfits, worn only two or three times at most? In the age of social media, there's no room for repeats. Even if a celebrity dares to wear the same saree or carry the same purse twice, they become easy targets for online trolling.

Here's the real twist: the sustainability movement needs to take centre stage in our homes. We need a serious fashion revolution. When my daughter got engaged in December 2022, I decided to shake things up — no dress code!

Some asked why, and my response was as simple as a fashionista's aversion to last season's trends: Wear something that keeps you warm in December. There was no need to drain wallets or contribute to fashion's environmental impact for my event.

Unless we're okay with our great-great-grandchildren celebrating Christmas in 40-degree heat, we need to start making changes now. We're not just fashionably late; we're dangerously late. It's time for a collective commitment to turn away from excess and embrace a new mindset: use, reuse, repair, recycle, and reduce. Let's ditch fast fashion and make sustainable style the next big trend.

CHAPTER 90

VACATION – OVERTOURISM

Everyone is on vacation, so I'm not expecting many readers. Let me take a moment to share my thoughts. I was planning a family vacation, but we encountered a series of hurdles.

India was too hot and humid, Europe made visa processes a hassle, the USA would throw off our schedules with jet lag, Africa had already been ticked off, and places like Thailand and Malaysia lacked enough vegetarian food options. As for package tours? They felt far too restrictive.

After crossing off all these possibilities, we made a simple decision: stay home. Instead of running around from place to place, we're enjoying quality family time right here. Honestly, vacations are overrated and overhyped. They're often exhausting, and instead of leaving you rejuvenated, they can drain you. The irony of needing rest after a vacation says a lot. I've never been a fan of those kinds of holidays.

As vegetarians, finding suitable food while traveling adds another layer of complexity. Hunting for the right places to eat turns into a project of its own, consuming both time and energy.

The whole vacation hype is driven by airlines, hotels, and travel companies pushing an agenda: making us feel like we **'need'** to travel to complete some imagined bucket list. It's their business, after all. And if you really think about it, most tourist destinations blend together—same beaches, same mountains, similar city landscapes whether you're in Europe or America.

Tourism, in my view, is overrated. Social media amplifies this pressure, pushing people to fall into the trap of thinking they need to travel to be fulfilled.

In India, there's a huge craze to travel abroad, partly because we don't value our own tourist spots. With a bit of civic sense, India could easily become one of the world's top destinations, but sadly, that's not the case.

As for me, I live in a beautiful, sea-facing house. With that kind of view and a good book, there's absolutely no reason for me to step out for a vacation. Quality time with myself and my loved ones is all I need.

CHAPTER 91

LOAN (DEBT)

My associate, from India, sent me some fascinating articles about good debt versus bad debt and sought my thoughts on the topic. My father was a modest yet successful businessman who adhered to a single principle: never borrow money. I followed his lead and have always avoided taking on loans. My only credit card has a minimal limit.

My investment philosophy aligns with this principle. I avoid companies with excessive debt. Will they prioritise paying interest or dividends to shareholders? Unlike younger generations, I can't fathom taking a loan for a luxury item like the latest iPhone or a vacation. To me, it's akin to spending future earnings in the present. I only ever took out a loan for a vehicle, and even then, it felt like a necessity.

Claims of 0% interest are misleading; processing fees often exceed the interest rate. Middle-class families may find it difficult to avoid housing loans due to soaring real estate prices. However, I would opt to live in a rented home until I could afford a down payment of at least 70%.

A colleague of mine recently faced a financial setback. She secured a loan at a low interest rate in the Middle East, used the funds to purchase a home in India, and lost her job within six months. Unfortunately, she's unable to return to her previous country without repaying the loan in full, and she can't sell the unfinished flat.

For business owners who can generate post-tax returns of 13-14%, taking on debt at 7-8% might be a strategic move. However, as a non-business owner, I prefer to avoid leverage and rely solely on my own funds for investments.

In essence, I strive to avoid alcohol, unnecessary commitments, and debt.

CHAPTER 92

INDIA – INVESTMENT DESTINATION

India never ceases to surprise me. After navigating through rain, floods, and chaos, I landed at AMD airport, where the exit process was incredibly smooth. Within just 45 minutes, I was through immigration, had my baggage, and was in a taxi.

There's an undeniable entrepreneurial spirit in India. Everyone seems to be building something. My cab driver, for instance, told me about an app he's developing that connects people with mechanics at any time for car services. I wished him the best of luck. Before my trip, the news was filled with stories about heat waves in India, so I came prepared. But to my surprise, the temperature in AMD was a manageable 36°C, and the evenings were quite pleasant.

It feels like everyone in India is an investor. In every corner, there's a mini Rakesh Jhunjhunwala, eager to offer stock tips. Having been an NRI for over 20 years, I can't help but wonder — am I the one who's truly lacking?

Meanwhile, watching our foreign ministry stand up to the EU on election matters and call out the US on violence in universities was a pleasant surprise. In the past, we would meekly accept criticism from Western media, but now, India is strong enough to push back and remind them to mind their own business.

Overall, India's future looks incredibly bright. There's so much talent and hardworking people here. If we can manage people's aspirations, maintain religious harmony, and instil a bit more civil discipline and patriotism, I believe there's no turning back.

I'm invested in India — Are you?

CHAPTER 93

FREEBIES

I pulled into the petrol station, smoothly opened the tank lid, and rolled down the windows with practiced ease. "Special, full tank, and card payment," I muttered, following the usual pump routine.

While lost in thought, mentally preparing for my next big meeting, a voice interrupted, "That'll be AED 380, sir."

"Whoa, that's steep! Any chance of a discount?" I asked without thinking.

The attendant burst out laughing. "Sir, in 20 years of working here, no one's ever asked for a discount! Which planet are you from? But hey, download our app, and you'll get a free coffee and doughnuts next time."

Ah, the relentless negotiator in me never takes a break. When strategic procurement hits a wall, I turn to haggling for discounts. And if that doesn't work? I'm all about scoring those extras — free services, free parts, extended warranties. It's always about squeezing in a little something extra!

CHAPTER 94

FINANCIAL EDUCATION

Other day, while talking to a colleague, he casually mentioned that most of his savings were tied up in bank fixed deposits and real estate. I was surprised. If this is the situation of an educated individual, what about others?

Most Indians tend to invest in just these two asset classes because they are risk-averse and don't want to hire financial consultants, fearing the cost.

I explained to my colleague that fixed deposits aren't ideal investments. If someone says engineers don't understand finance, that's not entirely accurate. Many IIM graduates start as engineers, and numerous CEOs and MDs responsible for profit and loss statements are also engineers. So, to claim engineers don't understand finance isn't correct.

However, aside from these high-ranking professionals, do most engineers understand personal finance? My experience suggests that many don't, and as a result, they often find themselves in financial difficulties.

After running the numbers, I had to explain to him that these investments weren't even keeping up with inflation. His response? "I don't understand finance."

If you don't understand finance, seek help from a professional financial planner. This will ensure you're prepared for your retirement, your children's education, and even potential job loss if it ever happens.

Financial Education must be part of every curriculum!

CHAPTER 95

PARENTAL FAULT LINES — I

As per the recent study cost of raising a child in India based on current rates, is approximately 67.5 lakhs. If the child chooses to pursue a degree in the UK or the USA, a common aspiration among many students today, this figure can climb to a staggering 2 crores.

Furthermore, Indian parents often invest significantly in their children's weddings. On average, a middle-class family spends six times their annual income on this event, which translates to around 50 lakhs at current prices.

Considering these factors, the total cost of raising a child until marriage can exceed 2.5 crores, especially if they pursue foreign education and have a grand wedding. For families with two children, this figure doubles to 5 crores. Do you possess sufficient savings and investments to meet these expenses?

Beyond the financial aspect, parents also endure countless sleepless nights, stress, and provide unwavering moral support. In return, they often yearn for simple gestures, such as a daily phone call from their children. However, in today's fast-paced world, many children prioritise their careers and may not be able to dedicate the time needed to care for their parents in their old age.

Before you spend such amount of money please think:

1. Can you afford it?

2. Does your Son / Daughter wants to go abroad just because their friends are going?

3. Are you doing it just to impress others in society?

4. Are their suitable options available within India

Let me tell you that Education Overseas have become extremely expensive besides that chances of getting jobs are getting very remote. Unless, children are very talented getting job and settling down in foreign countries is not easy.

Please do not take loans or dig into your retirement funds. Children can take education loan.

My sincere advice to parents is to prioritise their own financial security and well-being before making significant investments for their children. It is crucial to ensure a comfortable retirement for oneself before attempting to build a future for the next generation.

Love your children but don't spoil them.

CHAPTER 96

PARENTAL FAULT LINES — II

It's a busy season for Indian students heading abroad for higher studies. According to a Business Standard report, Indian student spending overseas will reach USD 80 billion annually.

An average middle-class Indian parent spends around INR 70 lakhs to raise a child through graduation. If the child pursues foreign education, add another INR 1 crore, and for marriage, an additional INR 50 lakhs. The total cost comes to about INR 2.5 crore per child. For two children, this amounts to a budget of INR 5 crore.

But this only covers the financial aspect. Think about the countless sleepless nights, the endless queues you've stood in, the many birthday parties, and the sleepover dramas you've endured — all of which have an emotional cost that can't be quantified.

If parents can afford it, I would certainly encourage them to support their children. However, if they can't, it shouldn't come at the expense of their retirement savings or lead to loans they'll struggle to repay. In such cases, students should take out loans themselves and bear the responsibility of repayment.

I know many parents who make this huge emotional mistake. One of my distant relatives withdrew INR 50 lakhs from his small business to finance his son's foreign education. The son wasn't particularly bright, but his mother insisted on a foreign degree. The father managed to raise the money, but within two years, his business collapsed.

In another case, a businessman shut down a successful venture in his village and moved his family to Ahmedabad because his wife wanted their children to receive a top-notch English education in the city. He ultimately went bankrupt after failing to establish a new business there. As a financial advisor, I firmly believe that you must take care of yourself first. Ensure your retirement fund is secure. Make sure you have adequate health and life insurance.

No matter how well-educated or virtuous your children are, they may not return to care for you. They will have their own responsibilities and careers. Some may not even have time to call their parents.

Be careful. Don't let emotions lead you to make poor parenting decisions!

CHAPTER 97

ELDERLY CARE

Yesterday, while at the gym, I encountered an elderly woman who was working out with remarkable vigour. I was curious about the reason behind her intense workout, and she shared that she was alone and had no one to rely on in case of illness.

This encounter transported me back to my mother's last days in India, where my mother was fortunate to be surrounded by her children and extended family during her years of suffering. She was lovingly cared for by my brother and his family, as well as the rest of our relatives. In fact, she was treated with utmost care and attention, having nearly all her needs met.

However, when we gathered as a family to mourn her passing, a single question lingered in everyone's mind: Who would take care of us in our old age? This seems to be a pressing concern among people in their fifties and beyond, often discussed among friends and relatives.

Today's nuclear families, with one or two children, often lead to geographical separation. Children may move away from their parents' homes to pursue better career opportunities in different cities or even countries. In urban areas, accommodating parents in the same residence can be challenging due to the limited space available in small apartments, even with the best of intentions.

It's not solely about money. While financial planning can address material needs, the emotional aspect requires equal attention. Who will provide care when you are unable to move around or are confined to bed due to illness or injury? As long as you and your partner are both healthy, the situation is manageable. But what happens when you are alone without a partner or children?

I believe technology has the potential to connect elderly individuals and address their needs. Initiatives aimed at finding companions for the elderly or pairing them with younger individuals are commendable. However, these resources are often limited to larger cities, leaving rural areas underserved. Nevertheless, it's encouraging to see that someone is considering the needs of the elderly.

Let us all strive to be good citizens and care for our elders.

CHAPTER 98

DUBIOUS PHILANTHROPY

———◆———

A billionaire wants to donate all his wealth to charity. These are the same billionaires who:

- Haven't paid a penny in state taxes, thanks to top-notch lawyers.

- Have systematically crushed small competitors.

- Have monopolised their products and services, deceiving gullible customers.

- Have drained every last drop of energy from their employees.

Growing up in India, I witnessed this countless times. A wealthy businessman, Tarachand Sheth, made his fortune by lending money to the needy at exorbitant interest rates. If you repaid him on time, there was no issue. But if anyone defaulted, he made their life unbearable, stripping them of basic rights and dignity.

The irony? The same man would go to the temple and proudly donate 51 kg of ghee for the deity's anointing, 10 tolas of gold for the deity's jewellery, and more. He'd even outbid others for the honour of performing the aarti, just to capture the town's attention.

I see striking similarities between these uneducated village businessmen and highly educated billionaires.

Both are parasites of humanity.

Do you understand this kind of philanthropy? Or is it just a way to deceive God and secure a place in heaven?

CHAPTER 99

VACATION TO EUROPE

My first European vacation in July 2016 was a disaster. Europe was experiencing a massive heatwave, and to my surprise, most hotels didn't have air conditioning—or even fans. In 2020, I decided to try again and applied for a Norwegian visa.

Recently, the Indian passport improved its ranking by 5 positions, now occupying the 57th spot. As a proud Indian, despite having lived outside India for the past 20 years, I maintain a strong connection to my homeland through regular visits and active involvement.

However, my pride often falters when it comes to planning overseas vacations, especially to countries that require prior entry visas. Many nations impose this requirement, which can be a cumbersome and time-consuming ordeal.

A recent European visa experience was particularly frustrating. Despite waiting for a long time to get an appointment, the embassy held onto our family's passports for 22 days. This delay meant we had to cancel our travel plans just two days before departure due to strict cancellation policies.

When the visa was finally granted, it was only for 15 days—a stingy and almost disrespectful decision, considering the circumstances. Unfortunately, this kind of treatment is all too common for Indian citizens. It's their country, and if they choose not to welcome us, what can we do? Post-Covid, Europe is also dealing with the strain of over-tourism.

Many of my friends and family have come back from European vacations, full of praise for its systems, discipline, and natural beauty. That's all fine — until they start comparing India to Europe.

That's where I draw the line. To me, Europe is nothing more than a museum of wealth looted from across the world. Whether it's London, Paris, or Milan, their riches were plundered from Asia and Africa, and this stolen wealth was cleverly reinvested into the Industrial Revolution and education.

Take Switzerland, for example. For decades, it harboured trillions of dollars in 'dirty money' from corrupt politicians, drug lords, and arms dealers, all under the guise of banking secrecy. Was that wealth ever legitimate?

Let me steal a million dollars first, then I'll clean up my act — sounds familiar, right? Read history. Read books. Stop making false comparisons between India and Europe. This isn't a case of comparing apples to oranges — it's more like comparing watermelons to grapes.

CHAPTER 100

BLAME IT ON PARENTS

I asked my colleague why he had diabetes at such a young age. His response was, "It's genetic." I then asked, "But why do you eat so much sugar and junk food?" He replied, "That's how my mom used to feed me. My tiffin was always packed with Maggi noodles, and lunch was usually burgers. Only at dinner did I get daal chawal."

When I asked, "Why are you late to the office today?" he said, "My kids were watching TV late into the night, and I couldn't sleep. Plus, my wife stays up playing on her phone, which also disturbs my sleep."

I pressed further to my relatives Son, "Why are you spending so much money on your marriage while your own salary is so limited?" His answer: "What can I do? That's what my parents want.

"Don't buy house but rent it now and later buy it. You are unnecessarily getting into fixed asset while your job is not permanent – No – my parents want it. This is a mindset of constantly blaming parents, partners, or others for everything wrong in life. But at some point, you must take charge of your own life. Whatever your parents did, they had their reasons, but you can't keep blaming them forever.

If your parents have diabetes or high blood pressure, take it as a warning and make the necessary changes. Don't just blame genetics — take control and take action.

For example, both my parents had dental issues, so I started seeing a dentist regularly from the age of 25, and I get check-ups every year. My father had prostate issues, so I schedule an annual visit with my urologist. Your parents are giving you early warnings, and it's important to learn from them, take preventive measures, and stop using genetics or your upbringing as an excuse.

CHAPTER 101

DEADLY DEMENTIA

The other day, I heard one of my colleagues mother has Dementia. It's a devastating disease that causes a gradual loss of memory and cognitive function. Patients may forget simple tasks like eating or bathing, and unfortunately, there's currently no cure.

Imagine the impact on loved ones. When a family member suffers from Dementia, the entire household is affected. While we can plan for education, careers, finances, and other aspects of life, death is unpredictable.

My parents passed away from cancer in their eighties, and witnessing their suffering during the final stages was heartbreaking. Despite having access to medical care, their pain was unbearable.

If we could plan our deaths, we could approach life with a different perspective, perhaps focusing on the most meaningful moments.

Voluntary euthanasia might be a compassionate option for individuals who reach a certain age and are no longer able to care for themselves. This practice could potentially alleviate physical and mental suffering.

CHAPTER 102

PROBLEM OF PLENTY

Whenever I decide to watch something on Amazon or Netflix, I end up surfing for almost 30 minutes and watching nothing. There's just too much choice, and I get completely confused about what to watch. No AI has yet been able to recommend a plain, simple family comedy that suits my taste.

A colleague of mine is looking for a suitable match for her daughter. In India, there are so many options when it comes to choosing a groom. But her daughter can't decide — should she pick someone who lives in India or abroad, works in IT or as a doctor, looks smart or has a stable job, or perhaps someone who's a businessman? There are so many choices, and she's feeling overwhelmed. She's now over 30 and still undecided.

A friend of mine keeps talking about starting a SIP (Systematic Investment Plan). But he's utterly confused about where to begin. In India, there are 1,200 mutual fund schemes, and when you factor in the combinations, you're looking at 10,000 different options.

How do you choose? You need an expert to guide you. And it's not just about getting the highest returns — it's about understanding your risk appetite, your liquidity needs, and your financial goals.

It's hard to know which path to take without proper guidance!

CHAPTER 103

PARTNER TRAINING

I was at Kotak Bank last week when I saw an elderly couple step out of an auto and slowly make their way into the branch. They were clearly struggling, but the wife was doing her best to care for her husband. The bank manager had them sign a few documents, and they eventually received some money.

After they left, the manager turned to me and said, "The husband has dementia, and the wife knows nothing about banking."

He went on to explain that they are reasonably wealthy, but their children are all settled abroad. While their children have million-dollar packages, they seem indifferent to the millions of rupees their parents have here.

What a life! We spend our entire lives trying to upgrade the lives of our children, yet when we need them the most, they can't or won't compromise their careers to take care of us.

Dementia is a strange and heartbreaking disease. You don't die, but you lose a little bit of yourself every day. There's no cure, and no amount of money can truly help. Only close family members can provide the necessary care. Money can solve many problems, but it certainly can't solve them all.

It's crucial to ensure that your partner learns to manage everything independently — finances, banking, investments, driving, and more.

How much can you really trust a bank relationship manager? These managers change every 2–3 years. Just when you build a relationship, they move to another bank or location. It's better to have a personal financial advisor to take care of your finances in your later years.

We know it's our responsibility to care for our children until they can stand on their own feet, but when do children realise it's time to start caring for their parents?

CHAPTER 104

SMALL BUSINESS

One of the perks of being a Procurement Manager is the opportunity to meet a wide variety of people. And by "wide variety," I mean a delightful smorgasbord of humanity — when my schedule allows, of course. From entrepreneurs who've conquered the business world multiple times (and sometimes even cancer!) to Emirati businessmen sharing tales of struggle and triumph, and single moms turning tragedy into entrepreneurial success, my journey has been nothing short of inspiring.

In our discussions, we dive deep into their track records, experiences, annual turnovers, profitability, and all those fascinating business details. For large companies, a quick Google search usually reveals everything I need to know. But for small businesses, these face-to-face interactions are invaluable like playing business Sherlock Holmes, minus the deerstalker hat.

Now, here's where things get a bit humorous. My habit of asking about turnover and profitability has taken an unexpected and rather amusing turn. Imagine this: the other day, I walked into Al Madina to buy milk, and without thinking, I asked the cashier, "**Kitna dandha hota hai?**" (Translation: "What's your business turnover?"). The look on his face — a mixture of confusion, amusement, and disbelief was priceless.

It didn't stop there. The following week, during a massage session with my Keralite masseur, I was so relaxed that I absentmindedly asked, **"Kitna kar lete ho?"** (Translation: "How much do you make?"). He paused for a moment, probably wondering if he should knead that curiosity right out of me. And even my barber wasn't spared. Mid-haircut, I casually inquired about his daily earnings. His scissors hovered dangerously close to my ear as he mulled over my question.

The responses were mind-boggling! Al Madina pulls in AED 25,000 daily, the masseur earns AED 10,000, and the barber shop nets AED 2,500 each day. Multiply those figures by 360, and their annual turnovers make you wonder why anyone bothers with corporate life. While their profit margins aren't sky-high, the employment they generate is impressive.

When I eventually return to my hometown of Vadodara, my goal is to support independent businesses like these. Not for profit, but to help generate employment and give back to the community.

CHAPTER 105

INDIAN PARENTS

Indian parents express love in a unique and profound way. We go to great lengths to provide our children with the very best — enrolling them in top schools, sports clubs, tutoring sessions, and offering every opportunity within our means. We work tirelessly, often taking loans or dipping into our savings to secure their education and ensure a bright future.

However, in our eagerness to protect them from every hardship, are we unintentionally depriving them of vital life lessons? By clearing their paths of obstacles and shielding them from failure, could we be hindering their ability to build resilience and independence?

In contrast, many Western parents encourage their children to face challenges and embrace responsibility, allowing them to grow through their experiences and learn from adversity.

Our love is boundless, but perhaps it's time to reconsider our approach. Sometimes, the greatest gift we can offer our children is the opportunity to face and overcome challenges on their own, fostering strength and self-reliance.

CHAPTER 106

MARRIAGE ANNIVERSARY

First of all, I wonder why couple celebrating their 25th wedding anniversary! Initially, I wondered why we make such a big deal about these milestones. After all, in cricket-obsessed India, we don't celebrate reaching a quarter-century with the same enthusiasm as we do a full century. But the more I thought about it, I realised that celebrating 25 years of marriage is very much like celebrating a century in cricket — it's not about just staying in the game, but about navigating the challenges and triumphs over time.

Think of it this way: If we assume the couple had four disagreements, or "vivaads," each year, that's a total of 100 vivaads over 25 years—much like a century in cricket! A "vivaad" isn't just a simple argument; it represents moments when communication (samvad) breaks down. However, what sets Indian marriages apart is the ability of couples to resolve these conflicts and compromise. Compromise is the glue that holds many Indian relationships together, allowing them to push through the bumps in the road and emerge stronger.

After hundreds of such disagreements and reconciliations, each partner becomes an expert in understanding the other. They accumulate a vast database of knowledge about each other's preferences, moods, and dislikes. Over time, this knowledge becomes second nature. With each disagreement resolved, they learn more about how to handle each other, creating a deep reservoir of mutual understanding and wisdom. This database of experiences and resolutions becomes the foundation for a harmonious future together, providing them with the tools to navigate whatever comes next.

In Indian marriages, especially those arranged by families, couples often enter the relationship blindfolded. Unlike the Western dating model, many of us don't have much prior knowledge about our partner's temperament, habits, or personality before marriage. Personally, I've never been very lucky at card games like Teen Patti, where drawing the right card is left to chance. Similarly, when we marry, there's an element of chance involved—drawing a "Badshah" or "Queen" may not happen immediately.

Yet, after 25 years of marriage, the blindfold is long gone. By this time, the couple knows each other's strengths, weaknesses, and quirks intimately. They've built something far more valuable than luck—they've built understanding, respect, and a deep bond that allows them to thrive.

As the couple celebrates their silver jubilee, they are also entering a new phase of life—the second inning. With children grown up and often living abroad in countries like the UK or USA, the focus shifts back to the couple. This is a time when accumulated wisdom (gyan) from the first 25 years comes into play. They now have the experience and insight to fully enjoy each other's company, free from the distractions and responsibilities that once consumed them. It's not just a continuation of the journey; it's the start of a new, more profound phase where they can truly savour the partnership they've built.

So, here's to the next inning! May the lessons learned and the love nurtured over the past 25 years guide the couple toward an even more fulfilling future together.

CHAPTER 107

HUM DONO

I have known this couple, Suresh Bhai & Sarita Bhabhi for the last 20 – 30 years, rather more. I am not going to reveal my age in the process.

I did not think they were a happy couple when both were working till their late fifties. Suresh Bhai got V RS at age of 55 from the position of Bank Manager and a year later wife retired from position of School Principal.

Today Sarita Bhabhi is 75 and Suresh Bhai is 80 year old both living together with so much of love around, each one taking care of each other. Both suffer from some ailment or other but are able to do their household chorus.

I was surprised. How come there is so much love? Both shunned egos which their positions gave them as Bank Manager and School Principal. Whatever you do, your professional attributes definitely pip into your personal life as well.

Earlier, Kids were all around and they were busy managing work, life and kids. Now they are just all alone. Kids have settled in USA / UK. They hardly have time to meet parents as they are busy with their own careers and family.

Sarita Bhabhi told me, bhai, we are just all alone. Everyday night – I just check by keeping my finger toward his nose whether he is alive. If I lose him – I will be all alone but I don't want to lose him. What will I do all alone? If anyone of us dies, we will be miserable. We just want to die together.

From hating each other to love each other to the extent of dying together. Have you seen any such turnaround story? I have seen turn around in the industry, a company making 500 million USD profit is not now making 500 million losses, but this one is unique.

CHAPTER 108

CELEBRATION OF SILENCE

Typically, this time of year — spanning Navaratri to Diwali is filled with dance, music, parties, and gatherings. However, the Covid-19 pandemic altered these plans, prompting me to use this period for a completely different purpose.

I decided to take up VIPASSANA meditation for 10 days, practicing noble silence. No phone, no internet, no communication with the outside world. (It's especially challenging after the initial 2-3 days.)

This practice offers a profound opportunity to reconnect with oneself, allowing you to truly listen to your body and mind.

In today's world, one of the hardest tasks is to focus on a single activity at a time. We are constantly multitasking — juggling team meetings, emails, social networks, and WhatsApp messages simultaneously. This often leads to fragmented attention and unproductive outcomes.

Now more than ever, we must train our minds to concentrate on one thing at a time, aiming for a focused effort to achieve meaningful results. Human attention is a valuable resource giving and receiving 100% of it is a challenge in itself.

Daily meditation has become a necessity. I encourage you to embrace it as soon as possible, before life throws new challenges your way.

Stay happy, stay healthy, and start your journey with daily meditation.

CHAPTER 109

FOOD VS PHARMA

My favourite investment areas are food and pharmaceutical companies. Given the essential nature of these industries, they are relatively immune to economic downturns.

In recent months, the stock market has seen a general uptick, but drug companies specialising in obesity reduction, **such as Ozempic and Wegovy, have experienced particularly significant growth.** For instance, Eli Lilly's stock price has risen from $384 to $588 in just six months (a 54% increase), while Novo Nordisk, Europe's largest pharmaceutical company, has seen a 20% increase in its share price during the same period.

The driving force behind this surge is the development of groundbreaking obesity reduction drugs. These medications work by targeting specific hormones that regulate hunger and appetite. Despite their high current cost, the market for these drugs is estimated to be worth billions of dollars, according to Bloomberg.

The medical community widely recognises the effectiveness of these drugs, which could potentially become as commonplace as aspirin or blood pressure medication. The growing popularity of these drugs is further fuelled by celebrity endorsements.

However, the development of such anti-obesity medications poses a significant challenge to the food industry. If people are less hungry, who will consume excessive amounts of ice cream, chips, chocolate, pasta, pizza, and burgers? While food companies may not face extinction, their revenue and profitability could be adversely affected.

The ensuing battle between pharmaceutical and food companies will be a fascinating spectacle. Time will tell whether one industry will dominate the other, or if both will coexist at the expense of the average consumer.

Ultimately, the most effective way to lose weight is through a combination of reducing calorie intake and eating more slowly. Don't be swayed by the marketing efforts of food and pharmaceutical companies.

CHAPTER 110

INDIAN EDUCATION

Many average students in India often end up becoming college professors, commonly titled "Assistant Professors" in private institutions. While they're officially responsible for teaching, many of these professors are actually focused on preparing for competitive exams like UPSC, GMAT, or CAT to further their own careers. Teaching, in many cases, becomes a secondary concern.

Students, on the other hand, are "forced" into classrooms due to the rigid 75% attendance rule imposed by most colleges. This creates a cycle where students are stuck learning from professors who may not be genuinely invested in teaching. As a result, we end up with teachers who lack passion and students who lack interest, creating a disengaged academic environment.

The consequence of this system is a widespread gap in practical knowledge and skills among graduates. Many finish their degrees unprepared for the job market, lacking the real-world competencies required to succeed.

Meanwhile, Indian students flock to universities abroad—in Europe, the USA, and Canada—where they receive a better-quality education. Indian parents are spending enormous sums of money on foreign education, draining valuable foreign exchange. If we invested in improving our own universities, we could retain this talent, strengthen our workforce, and provide students with the opportunity to work within their own country and region, without needing to seek education or employment abroad.

India's higher education system needs a major overhaul, one that prioritises practical application, passionate teaching, and real-world skills, rather than merely fulfilling academic formalities.

CHAPTER 111

MICHHAMI DUKKADAM

Please forgive me if I have hurt you, knowingly or unknowingly, and I forgive all those who have hurt me. This one festival should scale upto a global scale for global peace.

This simple act is such a powerful way to free ourselves from jealousy, stress, competition, and envy, while also reconnecting with old friends, relatives, and business partners. I still wonder why this concept hasn't become an internationally celebrated day like Valentine's Day or Father's Day.

Jainism offers many fundamentally sound and scientifically backed principles, such as vegetarianism, non-violence, meditation, and forgiveness.

I hope the world soon embraces the teachings of Buddha, if not the religious aspects, then at least the values. This would undoubtedly make the world a better place.

We dream of settling humanity on Mars, yet we don't put enough effort into healing Earth—the planet that has sheltered us for millions of years.

Michhami Dukkadam, dear Earth. We humans are wired to be selfish, constantly living for the future instead of appreciating the present.

CHAPTER 112

MONEY & ME — FINDING THE BALANCE

Money is undeniably important to me, but it's not everything. I believe that money earned at the cost of family time, personal health, and mental peace isn't worth it. Here's why:

Time:
I've seen couples working in Big Tech and consulting firms clocking 12-hour days, six days a week. They hardly have time to connect with each other, lost in the whirlwind of office tasks, personal ambitions, and financial goals. Their lives feel like a relentless race, where even weekend gatherings are carefully scheduled. This isn't the life I want. I value my "me time" – those precious moments to pursue what I love, free from constant demands. As Mohandas Karamchand Gandhi wisely said, "There is more to life than increasing its speed."

Health:
The relentless pursuit of money often leads to neglecting one's health. People fall prey to lifestyle diseases like high blood pressure and cholesterol. The young may have the energy but lack the funds, while the older may have the money but lack the vitality to enjoy it. I've seen people unable to indulge in simple pleasures

because their health limits them. We need to prioritise our health to truly savour life. I once met a young woman who had to take melatonin even on vacation just to sleep – a stark reminder of how stress takes its toll. As Swami Vivekananda said, "The greatest religion is to be true to your own nature. Have faith in yourselves."

Mental Peace:

Take my politician friend, for example. He sleeps every night on a fortune of 50 crores, all earned without paying taxes. He can't deposit it in a bank, living in constant fear and paranoia. Many professionals compromise their ethics in pursuit of wealth, sacrificing their integrity and peace of mind. Even small perks, like a free coffee in the supply chain, come with strings attached. This is not the path I wish to follow. As the Dalai Lama poignantly observed, "Man sacrifices his health in order to make money. Then he sacrifices money to recuperate his health."

In conclusion, while money is important, it should never overshadow the true essence of life. Striking a balance between financial goals and personal well-being is essential for a fulfilling life. As Dr. A.P.J. Abdul Kalam said, "We should not give up, and we should not allow the problem to defeat us."

CHAPTER 113

KANJOOS

In my close circle of friends, I'm known as the most **Kanjoos** (miser) person. Personally, I believe I have a very decent lifestyle. While I don't drive a BMW or Mercedes or follow big brands, financial freedom has always been my primary goal. Moreover, my profession of finding quality items at lower prices has contributed to my ability to get more for less.

During the early 1990s, when I joined India's largest EPC company, I planned to retire from there. However, fate had other plans. The company began laying off employees around the year 2000, sending a stark warning to me and many of my friends. Without a secure income or substantial savings, we faced the daunting prospect of being unable to support our families.

Fortunately, my next assignment was an international posting to Japan. As a single person, I was able to save a significant portion of my salary. I immediately invested in an apartment and haven't looked back financially since. Saving a substantial amount of money has become a habit, and I achieved financial freedom at the age of 45.

My advice to young professionals will always be —

- Save more and spend less.

- Have an alternative source of income, either through investments or your partner's employment.

- Create a financial plan early in life.

By the age of 40, you should aim to achieve financial independence, so you're not solely reliant on your job for daily necessities. Proper financial planning is essential.

CHAPTER 114

FINANCIAL FREEDOM

Why Pursue Early Financial Freedom?

Financial independence doesn't imply complete cessation of work; rather, it signifies a freedom from necessity. You're no longer compelled to work solely to cover your expenses.

This newfound freedom allows me to reject demanding bosses, unreasonable clients, and unethical requests. It empowers me to make informed choices and exercise control over my time. The greatest wealth is not monetary but personal freedom and liberty.

How to Achieve Financial Independence:

- **Live within your means:** Spend less than you earn. Prioritise saving, ensuring that at least 30% of your income is invested.

- **Delay gratification:** Avoid unnecessary expenses like luxury cars, extravagant homes, expensive jewellery, lavish parties, and costly vacations.

- **Develop multiple income streams:** Explore opportunities such as rental income from commercial properties, royalties from digital content, or book sales.

- **Invest in yourself:** Continuously upgrade your skills and seek out new opportunities.

- **Prioritise health:** Take care of your physical well-being through regular exercise and a healthy lifestyle. Reduce healthcare costs by maintaining good health.

CHAPTER 115

BAHUBALI RETURNS

As stock markets worldwide continue to surge, investors are expecting significant returns on their investments. While investments in stocks and mutual funds can serve as a passive source of income, even for professionals, there is a noticeable lack of financial literacy among the general public, including many professionals.

In India, only 2% of the population invests in the stock market, compared to 50% in the United States. Fixed deposits and gold remain the favoured investment options for Indians, but this represents a missed opportunity for financial growth.

Recent estimates suggest that Indians hold around USD 350 billion worth of gold in their homes. If this wealth were redirected into productive business ventures, the country might not need foreign investments.

While the government is running online competitions to test public knowledge about topics like cows (a questionable use of public funds), similar initiatives to assess and improve financial literacy could have a far more meaningful impact on society and the nation.

Stay happy, healthy, and keep investing in profitable businesses — especially if you don't have one of your own.

CHAPTER 116

PSYCHOLOGY OF FREE

As a supply chain professional, getting something for free is always tempting. The other day, I went to a petrol station to fill my tank and noticed an advertisement for free nitrogen for car tires at a nearby service station. Naturally, I headed over and got my tires filled.

Afterward, a technician approached me and said, "Sir, your tires are almost worn out. You must replace them; otherwise, you could have an accident."

I was a bit surprised but agreed, thinking that my frugality shouldn't lead to an accident.

The next time I visited the same service station, they offered free air again. After filling the tires, the technician claimed my brake pads were completely worn out and needed replacement.

This time, I caught on to the trick. I declined and went to the OEM service station instead. They assured me that my brakes were perfectly fine.

It became clear that the service station was offering "free" air in exchange for expensive, unnecessary repairs. Similarly, my bank relationship manager, who offered free financial advice, had been selling me inappropriate policies.

A few years ago, I hired professional financial services—but that came with a cost, not for free.

After using free platforms like Google, Facebook, and WhatsApp for all these years, the world has realised the true cost—our privacy. In short, nothing is truly free. Especially when it comes to free advice, it's best to stay cautious.

One exception to this rule is Zerodha Varsity, which offers free financial education with no strings attached. Ironically, because it's free, I haven't completed the course yet, despite finishing a lesser-quality course that I paid for in USD.

The psychology of "free" isn't hard to understand. You just need to be cautious!

CHAPTER 117

SKIN IN THE GAME (SITG)

Since SEBI issued a circular mandating that 20% of the total annual salary, including bonuses, of key personnel at AMCs must come from the mutual fund schemes they manage, the phrase "skin in the game" has become a buzzword.

Coincidentally, I had just finished reading Nassim Nicholas Taleb's book Skin in the Game. The book is unconventional and tackles complex issues, claiming that much of the world is run by bureaucrats and politicians who have "no skin in the game" (NSITG). They are unaffected by the consequences of the decisions they make. Look no further than India's current situation.

My IIM-graduate General Manager committed to management that we would release 50 purchase orders within a week. This GM had never made a single purchase order himself — classic example of NSITG.

I also have a friend who watches IPL matches year after year yet doesn't know the difference between third man and fine leg fielding positions—another instance of NSITG.

When your employees start saying, "It's not my money, it's the company's money" — believe me, they have no skin in the game and won't be long-term assets for your organisation.

On the other hand, there are leaders who treat every penny spent as if it were their own, weighing every decision carefully. These are the ones who truly have skin in the game.

So, what kind of employee are you for your organisation?

CHAPTER 118

BUYER BEHAVIOUR

My father owned a small clothing shop, and naturally, it wasn't a fixed-price store. Bargaining and haggling over prices were common, and it was actually quite fun. I would often help out at the shop during my vacations.

There was one particular family that frequently visited our shop. They would look at dozens of sarees, try them on, but never actually buy anything. It was frustrating to see so much effort go to waste. Once, they did purchase a pair of undergarments, but they returned twice — once to exchange them for size and again for colour.

Knowing their history, the next time they visited and asked about prices, we quoted them three times the usual rate. This way, we could spend less time on them and focus more on our loyal customers.

The same principle applies to other businesses as well. Sending frequent inquiries without giving actual business is a waste of time, and you might end up receiving less competitive offers.

This serves as a clear reminder to examine your behaviour both before and after placing an order!

CHAPTER 119

PERSONAL FINANCE — EMERGENCY CALL

In the middle of nowhere, I received a call from my friend, asking to meet at Saravana Bhavan. I suggested discussing over the phone, but he insisted on meeting in person.

I was surprised. This man, accustomed to coffee at Dubai Mall or Burj Al Arab, was suddenly calling me to a humble eatery. He worked at a senior level in sales and marketing for an oil and gas company.

He explained that he had lost his job and urgently needed 50,000 AED to pay his child's school fees. I hesitated as I'd been in similar situations before and knew that once you help someone, the money is often lost. I'd lost money in many such instances.

I helped him with 10,000 AED and crowdfunded the remaining 40,000 AED, paying it directly to the school. However, I wondered why he was in such a dire situation despite his high salary. The problem was that personal finance isn't taught in schools. His expenses were exorbitant, his savings were meager, and most of his savings were tied up in real estate. He was trying to sell his properties, but distressed sales were yielding little.

Here are my tips for financial management:

- Save at least 30% of your salary monthly. Pay yourself first.

- Minimise unnecessary expenses. No one will remember your Rolex.

- Plan your life goals. Have specific investments for each goal.

- Start early. Ideally, begin in your late 20s. Compound interest is powerful.

- Avoid debt. Refrain from credit card loans under any circumstances.

- Invest in equity and debt funds based on your risk tolerance. If you're unsure, consider index funds.

- Continuously learn. Make investment mistakes, but learn from them.

- Invest in upscaling. Your current skills may become obsolete.

- Remember, your children are not your insurance policy, and you are not their bank. Plan for retirement wisely.

- Remember: No money, no honey, no friends, no relatives. Financial security is essential.

CHAPTER 120

HUMAN PSYCHOLOGY — NEWTON

Even though I've been an investor for the past 15 years (with a total portfolio of INR 4,60,000, which admittedly gives me bragging rights among my Gujju friends for owning a Larsen & Toubro, Reliance, and Asian Paints), I was unaware of this 300-year-old story and thought it would be interesting to share.

In early August 1720, Sir Isaac Newton sold his remaining safe investments to purchase shares in the South Sea Company. Since January of that year, shares in the company — one of the largest private enterprises in history—had increased eightfold, creating paper fortunes for thousands.

Newton profited handsomely, earning GBP 20,000. Even after selling his shares, the price continued to rise, leading him to reinvest the entire GBP 20,000 in hopes of becoming a multi-millionaire. By August, he had liquidated most of his bonds, converting them and other assets into South Sea shares.

Unfortunately, this proved to be a disastrous decision. Within three weeks, the market took a sharp downturn. By Christmas, the market had completely collapsed. Newton's losses amounted to millions of dollars in 21st-century currency. This incident underscores the fact that even a mind as brilliant as Newton's could succumb to greed. To succeed in the stock market, intelligence alone is not sufficient.

What truly matters is proper asset allocation, patience, and the guidance of a qualified advisor. It's akin to attempting to climb Mount Everest without proper training from a professional mountaineering school or the assistance of highly skilled local Sherpas.

The choice is yours. **Hire an expert, or follow in Newton's footsteps!**

CHAPTER 121

RETIREMENT PLANNING

One of the most common mistakes people make during retirement planning is investing their entire corpus in low-risk options like Fixed Deposits (FDs), Senior Citizen Savings Schemes (SCSS), or Post Office schemes. This can lead to a significant decrease in purchasing power over time due to inflation.

For instance, if someone retires at 60 with a retirement corpus of ₹1 crore, and assuming a life expectancy of 85, they would need to spend approximately ₹4 lakhs per year to sustain their lifestyle.

A more effective strategy, often recommended by financial experts, is to diversify your investments across multiple asset classes. This approach involves dividing your retirement funds into five buckets: the first three buckets should be invested in safe, low-risk options, while the remaining two buckets should be allocated to equity funds. However, for those unfamiliar with financial planning, it's advisable to seek professional guidance from a qualified financial advisor.

To illustrate this strategy, let's consider a retirement corpus of ₹1 crore. You could allocate ₹40 lakhs to safe investments like FDs, SCSS, or Post Office schemes for a period of 10 years. The remaining ₹60 lakhs can be invested in equity funds, but not all at once. To mitigate risk, consider investing this amount gradually over 2-3 years through Systematic Investment Plans (SIPs). If you're unsure about selecting specific mutual funds, investing in index funds is a relatively straightforward and often effective approach.

Remember, investing in mutual funds for at least 10 years can yield substantial returns. It's not rocket science; investing is a simple concept, but it's often overlooked in favour of the familiar, low-risk options like FDs.

Enjoy a fulfilling retirement! If you need assistance with retirement planning, consider hiring a trusted financial advisor.

CHAPTER 122

PERSONAL FINANCE

Why do Indian Seniors Die Rich but live mediocre life.

AED 500 for cosmetics? "We can't afford it," I exclaimed to my partner. Growing up in a middle-class Indian family, my family had always been frugal, carefully considering every expenditure. Dining out was a luxury, and even then, we'd gravitate towards the less expensive items on the menu.

These frugal habits were deeply ingrained in me. Even after working abroad in Japan and the USA, my stinginess persisted. In 2013, I met a financial advisor who assessed my finances and declared, "Sir, you're well-positioned for early retirement." My initial reaction was disbelief. "Nonsense," I retorted. "Do you understand inflation? Are you crazy?"

The advisor calmly explained that my expenses were significantly lower than my income, making early retirement a viable option. He suggested that if I wanted to continue working, I should increase my spending. This was one of the most unusual pieces of advice I'd ever received: "Spend more, sir...No need to save."

This encounter significantly changed my perspective. I began to spend extravagantly on things I truly valued while ruthlessly cutting back on unnecessary expenses.

It is not a bad idea to hire advisors, if you can afford them:

- Financial Advisor
- Dietician
- Personal Exercise Trainer
- Life Coach

This team can cater to your personal needs on a one-to-one basis, providing tailored solutions. Why should only celebrities have this privilege?

With digitalisation, it's easier than ever to access these services from the comfort of your home at affordable rates. The challenge lies in finding the right advisor, which often requires trial and error and is a less-traveled path.

We are all celebrities in our own right. We need to challenge ourselves to learn something new every day.

CHAPTER 123

JHUKEGA NAHI

During the Eid holidays, I finished reading Stock to Riches by Parag Parikh, a deep dive into investor behaviour. In my QPFP course, we had some lectures on the psychology of investor behaviour, but this book went further, explaining more aspects of behavioural psychology with additional examples. It was a pleasure to read a book rooted in Indian examples and context.

One of the behavioural traits discussed is the Sunk Cost Fallacy — where people struggle to let go of money already spent, often leading to further losses. Some examples include:

1. You buy movie tickets for your family worth INR 3,000, but it starts raining heavily. Despite the bad weather and traffic, you still go, enduring the inconvenience.

2. You enrol in a degree program, pay the fees, and realise the course isn't right for you, yet you spend the next four years completing it, wasting valuable time. (College dropouts like Bill Gates and Steve Jobs found greater success by leaving.)

3. You purchase a buffet dinner for INR 1,499 and overeat, disregarding the negative health effects just to get your money's worth.

Investors exhibit the same behaviour when they invest in certain stocks or funds. Instead of reassessing the market fundamentals, they keep buying to average down the price. Similarly, once we buy a flat or property and it doesn't appreciate after 3 to 5 years, we stay attached to it, paying maintenance fees, property taxes, and utility bills, all while waiting for the price to rise. We cling to the mindset of "**Jhukunga Nahi Saala. Apna price aayega!**" ("I won't bend. My price will come!")

However, this stubbornness doesn't serve investors or businesspeople well. By holding onto such beliefs, we are misleading young people, as this mentality is better suited to gangsters, not rational decision-makers. In reality, **Hum to roj Jhukate Hai** (we humble ourselves every day) — to our spouse, our boss, market conditions, the weather, nature, and even God. Sometimes, it's wiser to step back, reassess, and revise our decisions.

As financial advisors, our role isn't just to recommend the best stocks or funds but to help control investor emotions during market volatility, ensure proper asset allocation, and view the portfolio holistically!

CHAPTER 124

BANK OF FRUGAL

Hello Sharks,

You've probably heard of Laxmi Bank, which is present in every corner of India. But I'm the founder and director of Lukkha Bank — the Bank of Frugals.

Sharks, while every person with a bank account or credit card has a credit score, we issue a Carbon Credit Score based on their consumption patterns. The more you consume, the lower your carbon credit score.

Similar to how mutual funds pool our money and invest it in equities, we will pool carbon credits and exchange them with companies striving for net-zero emissions. We will sell our carbon credits to these companies in exchange for money, which will then be distributed to all unit holders. The only condition is that this money can only be used for physical and mental health purposes — not for increasing consumption.

Given that India has a large population with consumption levels far below the global average, we see immense potential in this business, especially when combined with the growing focus on health. This will give poor people worldwide an opportunity to earn money by consuming less and focusing on their health.

So, Sharks, are you ready to invest in Lukkha Bank with 100% equity for just INR 100? All we need is your guidance to make this concept go viral — and maybe someone like Kunal Shah or Nikhil Kamath to invest in the idea.

CHAPTER 125

MONEY MYTHS

"Money can't buy happiness, hunger, sleep, or love" — these are common myths in Indian society. The truth is, making money isn't easy, and earning it legally and ethically is even more challenging. But it's far from impossible.

Look at the returns provided by the Indian Stock Exchange this year:

- Nifty 50: 11.5%
- Nifty Mid Cap 150: 18.6%
- Nifty Small Cap: 19.3%

While these returns aren't guaranteed, with the guidance of a good advisor, you can achieve strong results. These are impressive numbers by any standard, yet only around 3% of Indians invest in the stock market.

Ironically, more people in India gamble on lotteries, online jackpots, and betting sites than invest in the market. Many seek shortcuts to quick wealth, rather than investing systematically in solid businesses.

And those who claim "money isn't important," or say things like Paisa ni koi kimmat nathi (money has no value) or Paisa hathno mail che (money is dirt on the hands), already have millions of dollars in their bank accounts before making such statements.

In reality, money can bring happiness—it can fund vacations, enable quality family time, provide access to education at prestigious institutions, and allow you to invest in yourself by hiring experts or starting a new business.

Start investing today with a long-term approach, perhaps through an SIP (Systematic Investment Plan). Now, let's address some common misconceptions:

1. **"Money doesn't buy happiness."**

    Actually, it does. How else would you afford overseas vacations, luxury hotels, or even trips to the movies without money? How can you access quality healthcare without financial resources? You need money—often a lot of it—to experience happiness.

2. **"Money can't buy comfort."**

    While money can't guarantee you'll sleep soundly, it can ensure that you have a comfortable place to sleep, a good bed, and a controlled environment. It can also free you from the worries that keep people awake at night.

3. **"Money will make you arrogant."**

    Not necessarily. Money amplifies who you already are. If you're kind, wealth will make you even kinder. If you're arrogant, it may enhance that arrogance. If you're enterprising, it will embolden you to take more risks and earn even more.

4. **"You don't need money to be educated."**

   True, intelligence can't be bought. But the best education in the world often comes with a hefty price tag. With money, you can hire coaches and mentors to help you reach your full potential.

5. **"Money can't buy love."**

   In reality, love often follows where money goes. This is a harsh truth of life, and everything else is a myth.

6. **"Spending money is bad."**

   Spending can also be an investment—especially when you invest in yourself. You can hire a personal development coach, a fitness trainer, or a relationship expert. You can also invest heavily in self-education.

In conclusion:

- Money does buy happiness.

- Spending money can be an investment.

- No one gets rich overnight.

- Money's real purpose is to set you free—not just to make you feel rich.

- Money won't change you—it will simply enhance who you already are.

CHAPTER 126

RETIREMENT

As an NRI, we frequently encounter the question: "Where will you retire, India or abroad?" For many years, my unequivocal response was India, primarily due to my birthplace and the presence of my friends and family.

India's abundant natural resources, majestic mountains, and pristine beaches, coupled with its thriving entrepreneurial spirit and booming economy, made it a compelling choice. The Sensex reaching new heights and the abundance of job opportunities, particularly in the oil and gas, engineering, and IT sectors, further solidified India's appeal.

However, as visa regulations have become more lenient overseas and financial security has increased, returning to India has become less straightforward for many of my friends. Despite our unwavering patriotism, the reality is that India's quality of life still falls short of many other countries.

High taxes often yield minimal returns, and even the affluent and educated lack basic community discipline. Apathy towards pet waste and disregard for parking regulations are common occurrences.

Yet, amidst this chaos, there is a unique harmony. The vibrant celebrations of numerous festivals, the delectable cuisine, and the cherished family bonds create an experience that is difficult to replicate elsewhere.

Ultimately, the decision of where to retire is a personal one, often influenced by one's birthplace and the place where one has built a career.

CHAPTER 127

ART OF LOSING MONEY

Indians are renowned for their savings habits, but their investment strategies often fall short. Moreover, Indians have a peculiar knack for losing money, continually discovering novel methods to deplete their finances.

For instance, did you know that approximately 2 million Indians lost a staggering 100 billion rupees in fraudulent cryptocurrencies? Additionally, millions of Indians are drawn to online gaming, often losing substantial sums in the process. New online gaming apps emerge daily, enticing young people with initial rewards before exploiting them financially.

Millions of Indians harbour the misguided belief that they will strike it rich through lottery winnings, while the entire lottery system is designed to generate profits for companies or states. Many individuals also fall victim to Ponzi schemes, where promised returns of double or quadruple their investment rarely materialise.

Our collective desire for quick profits and rapid results often leads us astray. Becoming a millionaire overnight is a pipe dream without proper planning, diligent work, intelligence, and sound business acumen.

If your goal is to achieve millionaire status, the most reliable path involves long-term planning and consistent investing.

What are your personal pitfalls when it comes to losing hard-earned money? **Start your investment journey today!**

CHAPTER 128

JOY OF COMPOUNDING

I have not changed my Barber, my Dentist, my Physician, my Financial Advisor & maid for last 10-15 years. I try to remain with same driver, same shop as far as possible. At times, I knew that person has taken advantage but he soon realises value of long term customer.

Yesterday, I completed reading "The Joy of Compounding" by Gautam Baid. This book delves into the principles of value investing, emphasising the importance of patience and continuous learning. It's a valuable resource for those seeking to build wealth through investments.

In my opinion, the principles outlined in "The Joy of Compounding" can be applied to various aspects of life, including health, relationships, and personal passions.

I once suggested to a friend who was experiencing back and knee pain that they start practicing yoga, as I had found it beneficial through my own long-term practice (thanks to a large EPC Company). Unfortunately, this advice backfired, as my friend experienced increased pain. While I had reaped the rewards of early investment in my health, my friend's experience highlighted the potential risks of applying a one-size-fits-all approach.

Just as running for an hour continuously is more beneficial than splitting it into two 30-minute sessions, the cumulative benefits of investment start to accrue after the initial investment period. Similarly, relationships require consistent effort and investment to yield lasting benefits. Expecting help from friends and family only in times of need is unlikely to be effective, as strong bonds are built through ongoing nurturing.

While practice may indeed make perfect, it comes at the cost of time, patience, and continuous learning. In today's fast-paced world, many people aspire to achieve wealth, health, and happiness overnight. However, there is no shortcut to success.

By investing in health, wealth, and relationships early in life, you can harness the power of compounding and achieve long-term fulfilment.

Compounding is '8th Wonder' and you will understand just by one simple example —

(1) $(1.01)^{365} = 37.78$

(2) $(0.99)^{365} = 0.0255$

CHAPTER 129

FINANCIAL SECURITY

More than Job Security, what you truly need is Financial Security! Financial security (FS) ensures that even if you lose your current job, you will still have enough money to cover essential needs like housing, food, and health insurance for the rest of your life.

Does financial security come automatically with a high salary? Not necessarily. Many well-educated professionals are unaware of how to make their hard-earned money work for them.

Here are a few tips from my personal experience:

1. **Choose a job that excites you and offers opportunities for learning rather than focusing solely on salary.** This investment in your growth will pay off in the long run.

2. **Keep your material aspirations in check.** Ensure they remain well below your income level, and start investing as early as possible.

3. **Avoid taking on debt, even if you can afford it.** Stay clear of credit cards and bank loans unless absolutely necessary.

4. **Invest in a diverse portfolio of stocks and mutual funds with a long-term perspective (10 years or more).** The power of compound interest will work in your favour.

5. **Seek advice from a professional financial planner if you're unfamiliar with investment strategies.** Avoid relying on free advice.

6. **Use your spare time to learn more about personal finance.** In both personal and professional life, the bottom line is what truly matters.

Stay healthy and secure — both physically as well as financially.

CHAPTER 130

FINANCIAL LITERACY

Growing up in India, I witnessed this firsthand with three or four relatives. They were once incredibly wealthy, living in big houses and driving fancy cars, but after some misfortune, their children are now working ordinary jobs.

"Laxmi is Chanchal," my father used to say, meaning wealth is fickle and doesn't stay with you for long—unless your values remain strong. He often spoke about the "third-generation curse," where 90% of wealthy families lose their fortune by the third generation.

Today on Twitter, I came across a similar Scottish phrase: "The father buys, the son builds, the grandson sells, and the great-grandson begs." In Chinese, there's a saying: Fu bu guo san dai (wealth doesn't survive three generations).

It's also worth noting that 70% of lottery winners go bankrupt within a short time. They lose it all. The same goes for athletes and film stars who become rich overnight but end up bankrupt just as quickly. Most of them take excessive risks — drugs, alcohol, and poor business decisions being the main culprits.

Why does this happen?

A lack of financial education and discipline. When money comes too easily, it's easy to squander. Drugs, alcohol, and bad business choices are the top reasons for financial downfall.

It's crucial to teach our kids the value of money and the importance of hard work. They shouldn't be handed everything on a silver platter. They should struggle to build their own careers, businesses, and wealth. There's no need to give them everything. Give them enough to stand on their own feet. The rest, you can enjoy or donate to charity as you see fit.

A friend once asked me, "Why are you worried? You're not even first-generation wealthy, and your fortune is peanuts."

CHAPTER 131

RETIREMENTALITY

My father was a shopkeeper, and he worked until the age of 80. Even after being diagnosed with cancer at 78, he continued working. It was only in the last six months of his life that he became bedridden. He had a purpose: to get up every morning and go to the shop.

On the other hand, my uncle, a government employee, retired at 60 and passed away at 62 from a heart attack. This doesn't mean that every shopkeeper lives to 80 or every government employee dies at 60. However, it reinforced my belief that you should work as long as you can. Never think of retirement.

The concept of FIRE — Financial Independence, Retire Early — is overrated. What do you do after retirement if there's no purpose left in your life? I've been financially independent for the last 10 years, yet I still work as hard as I can. It helps you navigate difficult bosses, if you ever have one.

Retirement is not easy. Shifting from an extremely busy office life to sitting on a sofa in front of the TV is a drastic change, and it requires a lot of mental preparation.

For me, work is more than a pay-check. It's an opportunity to prove my worth, a window to connect with the world, and a way to build a large social circle, especially in a country where I don't have many relatives. For me, work makes up 75% of my life, and I would love to continue working as long as I can.

If circumstances change and I'm forced to retire, I have a plan B (Financial Advisor) and plan C (Writer, Author & Trainer) — or perhaps all of them combined. If you're planning retirement, I highly recommend reading The New Retirementality by Mitch Anthony. It will open your eyes.

CHAPTER 132

MY INSURANCE MISTAKES

I consider myself educated, well informed, and well-travelled. On top of that I work in Procurement, so people assume I know everything about money. Honestly, most procurement engineers do not understand personal finance. But, how can we admit to the world?

In spite of all these credentials, I was royally fooled and mis-sold a host of insurance policies between 2003-2009 by my faithful (blood sucking) relationship manager.

- LIC–10 (Premium–INR 80,000) — Agent Uncle
- Axis-MetLife — 3 (Premium – INR 5,00,000)
- ICICI Prudential (Premium – INR 3,00,000)

None of these policies were suiting my profile. They were partly useful only if I die but not taking care of job loss or accident or loan liabilities. These were market linked plans which are hybrid of Insurance cum Investment but ultimately inflation adjusted returns were negligible (less than 3%). Moreover, as an NRI, I had no use from an Income Tax Point of view.

Most of the policies were having administration charges of 14 to 18% So almost 20% of the year premium is deducted in their admin charges. What returns will they provide? But, agents/ banks used to get 30% commission from the first premium. That's why they were pushing for these policies.

In 2013, when I hired a financial advisor, he did all the housecleaning and I started investing in plain term insurance, separate health insurance and SIP in mutual funds for investments.

Guys, Insurance is a very complicated subject. You and I don't easily understand which plan suits you perfectly. Even within the Financial Advisor Community there are specialists to handle this subject.

Just within Health Insurance there are 40 different types of plans and you will not understand what to buy? When you are under the impression that you have health insurance and when a real situation arises you will not get any benefits with some fine prints.

Like you need bespoke suits to meet your body dimensions, you need bespoke financial plan. This takes care of your Investment, Insurance, Retirement planning. Just don't buy some policies online as those are with minimum premium.

CHAPTER 133

REAL ESTATE MISTAKES

Every asset class has its golden period. Be it Gold, Equity or Real Estate. In India both real estate and Gold are being considered evergreen and as advised by so called free financial advisors, I started investing into real estate back in 2011.

1. I bought my first flat for investment in Gandhinagar, in 2015, considering it a Tier II city and Capital of Gujarat and with upcoming GIFT city, flat will appreciate very fast. Nothing of that sort happened. I was able to get one Tennent after a long wait and he was paying me rent of INR 9,000 involving lots of hassles of agreement and documents. When I recently sold the flat, my total annual return was less than 2% considering rental yield.

2. I also bought a piece of land in partnership in the industrial town of Maharashtra and gave it for the development to Builder in 2016. In 2018 he started construction. In 2020, Covid stuck. His project was stalled. Builder went Bankrupt. He has neither returned me my plot nor the flat promised. No sign of Builder getting revived and a big legal fight is looming in front of us.

3. Another prized piece of plot, I acquired in 2017 and I am trying to sell from 2020 onwards but not able to find Buyer yet. Buyers told me that there is no proper approach road left for my

property as surrounding builders have encroached on the land and your plot has no access.

I am trying to share my real estate mistakes so that you don't repeat it. Real Estate Investments may not be super successful, unless you do some deal in commercial property or Tier 1 cities which will have big ticket size and long gestation period.

I may be grossly wrong. Take your own call before investing into land, flats for investments.

With help of my financial advisors, I rebalanced portfolio to 70% Equity, 10% Debt Funds, 10% Gold and 10% real estate. This is so hassle free and you can have your money anytime you need it.

CHAPTER 134

ONE AND HALF MINUTE

Once while I was in India, I experienced an incident which I would like to share with you. I was in my hotel and had just entered the elevator when, shortly after it started moving, it abruptly stopped due to a power outage. The elevator, made by a reputable company, was completely enclosed and safe, but it was stuck.

One of the fellow passengers began shouting, grumbling, and jumping, expressing frustration about the reliability of the hotel & country. She increased her blood pressure and lost cool completely. In contrast, I was cool clam and used to it, I took out my phone and turned on the torch, providing some light in the situation.

After about 1.5 minutes, the power was restored, and we safely reached the ground floor. The attendant there explained that when there's a power cut from the grid, the emergency generator kicks in, but it takes a minute or so.

During the crisis, your reaction in those critical moments matters greatly. I remained confident, knowing that we were in a reputable hotel with a reputable elevator brand. I trusted that the staff were aware of the situation and would not abandon us and what you can do from Elevator? You must rely upon outside forces. It is beyond your circle of influence.

To illustrate this further, consider an example from Stephen Covey's book – 7 habits of highly effective people: when a snake bites you, do you waste time hunting the snake down, or do you head straight to the hospital for anti-venom dose?

In life, whether you're stuck in a car, facing challenges in your job, or dealing with a crisis in your marriage, your reaction during those brief moments of crisis determines the outcome. Stay calm, trust the process, and handle the situation with confidence.

CHAPTER 135

HAPPY RAMADAN

———•———

The soft chime of the doorbell echoed through the quiet morning, stirring me from my sleep. Confused by the early visit, I shuffled to the door, wondering who could be calling at such an hour on a weekend.

Opening the door, I was met with the unexpected sight of my Bangladeshi Car Cleaner standing on my doorstep. His presence took me aback, and I couldn't help but ask what had brought him here so early.

With a gentle smile, he explained, "Sir, I'm off to the airport soon. My flight leaves at 10 AM, but before I go, I wanted to see you."

I couldn't fathom why he had chosen to visit me, especially on a day of celebration like Eid, when I wasn't observing the festivities.

Before I could respond, he spoke again, his words carrying a weight of sincerity that touched my heart. "Sir, you've been so kind to me. I'll always remember your generosity. Not many people show us the care and compassion that you do."

With those heartfelt words, he turned to leave, leaving me standing there, overwhelmed by a flood of emotions.

As I watched him go, I couldn't help but reflect on the ways I had been able to support him. Beyond just paying his salary, I had offered him assistance in times of need, providing him with medicines and food when he fell ill or inviting him to share in our family celebrations.

In that moment, I realized the profound impact of simple acts of kindness. And as tears welled up in my eyes, I felt a deep sense of gratitude for the opportunity to make a difference in someone's life, even in the smallest of ways.

CHAPTER 136

AM I PERFECT?

For the outside world, I am perceived as a successful Supply Chain Director, earning a handsome salary. I'm also a writer, speaker, investor, and a person juggling multiple roles. To many, success is measured solely by the amount of money one earns, and by that standard, I am considered successful.

But does that mean I am flawless? Absolutely not!

I have my imperfections. I get irritated easily and struggle with controlling my anger. Despite undergoing anger management, I still find myself getting upset and angry from time to time. Every successful person has a hidden side that the outside world doesn't see.

Take Mohandas Karamchand Gandhi, for instance. While he shouldered the immense responsibility of leading the Indian National Congress, I'm sure his wife, Kasturba, his children, and close associates like Sardar Patel had to contend with a difficult person at times.

Similarly, Albert Einstein, one of the greatest minds of the 20th century, was an unfaithful husband and indifferent father. He divorced his first wife and neglected their disabled daughter. He once admitted, "For a man like me, there comes a decisive turning point in life after which you gradually lose interest in the purely personal and ephemeral side of things and channel all your efforts into the task of understanding."

One key element of success is single-minded focus, but this often comes at the expense of everything else. The hours spent working or traveling are also hours missed for your parent's doctor appointment, your child's dance performance, or a friend's anniversary celebration.

So, while I may appear successful to the outside world, the real heroes are those close to me, who endure my flaws, my anger, and my mood swings on difficult days. I owe so much to my family — my ever-silent wife, my endlessly understanding daughters, and my mother, who stood by me through every right and wrong moment.

www.ingramcontent.com/pod-product-compliance
Lightning Source LLC
Chambersburg PA
CBHW031610210526
45464CB00004B/1511